God's Word and Your World

 Think

 Ask

 Bible

God's Word and Your World

What the Bible says about Creation,
Languages, Missions and other Amazing Stuff

Laura Martin

CF4·K

Copyright © Laura Martin 2018

10 9 8 7 6 5 4 3 2 1

Paperback ISBN: 978-1-5271-0211-8

e-pub ISBN: 978-1-5271-0243-9

mobi ISBN: 978-1-5271-0244-6

Published by
Christian Focus Publications Ltd,
Geanies House, Fearn, Ross-shire,
IV20 1TW, Scotland.
www.christianfocus.com

Cover and internal page design by Pete Barnsley (Creativehoot.com)
Printed and bound by Bell and Bain, Glasgow.

Scripture quotations are from The ESV®Bible (The Holy Bible, English Standard Version®), published by HarperCollinsPublishers, ©2001 by Crossway. Used by permission. All rights reserved.

All rights reserved. No part of this publication may be reproduced, stored in a retrieval system, or transmitted, in any form, by any means, electronic, mechanical, photocopying, recording or otherwise without the prior permission of the publisher or a licence permitting restricted copying. In the U.K. such licences are issued by the Copyright Licensing Agency, Saffron House, 6-10 Kirby Street, London, EC1 8TS.
www.cla.co.uk

FROM THE AUTHOR TO YOU

My name is Laura Martin and I'm married to Bryan. We have five beautiful children and a crazy spaniel. I serve alongside my husband, who is pastor of River City Bible Church – a church we planted in Hamilton, New Zealand in 2010. Prior to that we were serving in a church in the U.K. I home-school our children, enjoy travelling, gardening, quilting, projects around the house, and writing. I love to disciple and counsel from God's precious Word. Thank you for reading!

Laura Martin

You can contact Laura at: laureemartin75@gmail.com

Dedication

Dedicated to my 'British parents'

Cyril and June Wearn.

Your example as a pastoral couple,
and your desire for young people and children
to come to know and trust in Jesus
through the Kingfishers Ministry at Alfold Chapel,
has been a blessing and an inspiration to many,
but most especially to us.

Contents

What does the Bible teach about...?

Chapter One
Creation 2

Chapter Two
The Fall 17

Chapter Three
Languages... 34

Chapter Four
Missions 53

Chapter Five
Charity... 74

Chapter Six
Society and Culture 89

Chapter Seven
The New Heaven and the New Earth 107

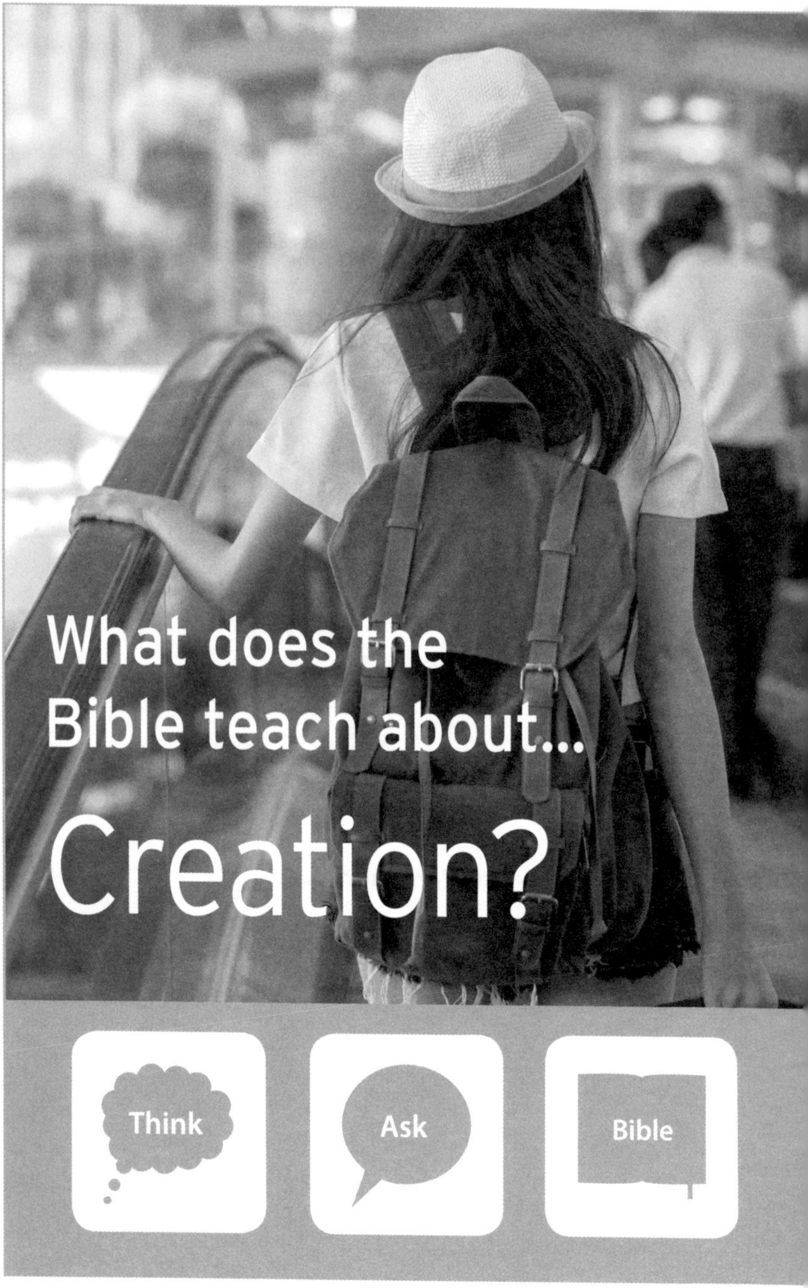

What does the Bible teach about...
Creation?

 Think

 Ask

 Bible

There is a battle that rages around us and has done for hundreds and hundreds of years. In fact, it is a battle so fierce that many have lost their lives over it, but the reality is that many are not aware of this battle. Many people will go about their daily lives not only unaware but perhaps at times even contributing to the cause of the battle, maybe without even realising it. Really? You might be amazed to think that, but it's true. So, what is this battle then, the one that we don't hear about on the news or read about in the papers? It's the battle for truth.

The battle began soon after the Lord God created this earth and everything in it. Something happened, something which you perhaps know to be called 'the Fall'. 'The Fall' describes Adam and Eve's first sin against God. It happened when Satan, in the form of a serpent, spoke to Eve to tempt her to eat the fruit from the tree which God had forbidden them to eat from. Satan said to Eve, 'Did God actually say …?' Satan wanted Eve to doubt God's words to her and her husband. And so began the battle for truth.

You may be thinking that this is all very interesting, but what does it really have to do with a chapter on what the Bible teaches about creation? Here's the thing. The Bible teaches that God created the world, and everything in and around it, in six days. Six actual days. That's amazing isn't it! But He is God. He is All Powerful. He is able to do far more than any of us could ever imagine He could do. But, there are many people today who deny God as Creator, and instead they choose to follow after Eve in believing Satan's lies. Perhaps they deny that it was six actual days of creation. Or perhaps they deny the way that God created, instead believing in a big bang or evolution. But here's the problem: When truth is denied in any form, God is dishonoured. Why? Because we read in Titus 1:2 that God is truth. And of course, the reality is that if we can't believe that the first three, or four, or five, or six chapters of the Bible are TRUTH, then how can we believe that any of the Bible is truth?

All Scripture is breathed out by God and profitable for teaching, for reproof, for correction, and for training in righteousness.

—2 Timothy 3:16

> ### Did You Know ...?
> Even the animals know their Creator:
> *But ask the beasts, and they will teach you; the birds of the heavens, and they will tell you; or the bushes of the earth, and they will teach you; and the fish of the sea will declare to you. Who among all these does not know that the hand of the Lord has done this?*
> —Job 12:7-9

The Bible says that all of Scripture is breathed out (spoken and authored) by God. Yes, God used men to write it down, but every single word in the Bible is from God. That means there are no errors and no contradictions. It is God's Word, from Him to us. And we read in 2 Timothy 3:16 that every word from God is useful in our lives. So, it's on that basis that we can confidently say that the account of creation in the Bible is literal (it happened exactly as it is recorded).

There's the battle for truth in a nutshell. It started back, way, way back, in the beginning. Speaking of beginnings, it does seem a very good place to start ...

Day One

In the beginning, God created the heavens and the earth. The earth was without form and void, and darkness was over the face of the deep. And the Spirit of God was hovering over the face of the waters.

And God said, 'Let there be light,' and there was light. And God saw that the light was good. And God separated the light from the darkness. God called the light Day, and the darkness he called Night. And there was evening and there was morning, the first day.

Here we have the very first day of creation. Now remember, God is Eternal. He has always been – there is no 'beginning' for God. Day one of creation marks only the beginnings of our world. On this first day God created the heavens and the earth. We also see that back on this first day of the creation week, the Holy Spirit was there too. What we don't see in these verses specifically, but we do see in other places of Scripture (John 1:1-3; Colossians 1:16), is that Jesus was also playing a major part in this wonderful creation week.

So, God spoke and commanded that there was light. He defined darkness and light, and He created night and day.

Day Two

And God said, 'Let there be an expanse in the midst of the waters, and let it separate the waters from the waters.' And God made the expanse and separated the waters that were under the expanse from the waters that were above the expanse. And it was so. And God called the expanse Heaven. And there was evening and there was morning, the second day.

On day two, we see a clear definition of sky around the earth. The waters are gathered and put into their place.

Day Three

And God said, 'Let the waters under the heavens be gathered together into one place, and let the dry land appear.' And it was so. God called the dry land Earth, and the waters that were gathered together he called Seas. And God saw that it was good. And God said, 'Let the earth sprout vegetation, plants yielding seed, and fruit trees bearing fruit in which is their seed, each according to its kind, on the earth.' And it was so. The earth brought forth vegetation, plants yielding seed according to their own kinds, and trees bearing fruit in which is their seed, each according to its kind. And God saw that it was good. And there was evening and there was morning, the third day.

On day three we see that the seas are gathered to specific places so that the dry land appears which enables growth. Day three brings with it things which grow from the ground: trees and plants and flowers and fruit trees and vegetables. This must have been absolutely beautiful to see, not growth over months and months but instant growth as the plants obeyed God's command to sprout, grow tall, bear fruit and produce seed for further growth!

Day Four

And God said, 'Let there be lights in the expanse of the heavens to separate the day from the night. And let them be for signs and for seasons, and for days and years, and let them be lights in the expanse of the heavens to give light upon the earth.' And it was so. And God made the two great lights—the greater light to rule the day and the lesser light to rule the night—and the stars. And God set them in the expanse of the heavens to give light on the earth, to rule over the day and over the night, and to separate the light from the darkness. And God saw that it was good. And there was evening and there was morning, the fourth day.

On day four God made the stars and the planets, the sun and the moon. All things which at night give light, and over the months and years give signs for seasons. These lights would even be a way that man and woman would navigate their way throughout the earth in days and years to come.

Day Five

And God said, 'Let the waters swarm with swarms of living creatures, and let birds fly above the earth across the expanse of the heavens.' So God created the great sea creatures and every living creature that moves, with which the waters swarm, according to their kinds, and every winged bird according to its kind. And God saw that it was good. And God blessed them, saying, 'Be fruitful and multiply and fill the waters in the seas, and let birds multiply on the earth.' And there was evening and there was morning, the fifth day.

On day five God filled the waters with creatures that swam and wiggled and splashed and frolicked! Enormous creatures which would seem to slowly push through the waters, lithe creatures which would be known for their speed and agility, teeny creatures who live in the depths of which human eyes would not see for thousands of years. Also on this day God created birds! Birds that trilled and sang and swooped and glided, waddled and swam and bathed in the sun. Can you even imagine it?

Day Six

And God said, 'Let the earth bring forth living creatures according to their kinds—livestock and creeping things and beasts of the earth according to their kinds.' And it was so. And God made the beasts of the earth according to their kinds and the livestock according to their kinds, and everything that creeps on the ground according to its kind. And God saw that it was good. Then God said, 'Let us make man in our image, after our likeness. And let them have dominion over the fish of the sea and over the birds of the heavens and over the livestock and over all the earth and over every creeping thing that creeps on the earth.' So God created man in his own image, in the image of God he created him; male and female he created them. And God blessed them. And God said to them, 'Be fruitful and multiply and fill the earth and subdue it, and have dominion over the fish of the sea and over the birds of the heavens and over every living thing that moves on the earth.' And God said, 'Behold, I have given you every plant yielding seed that is on the face of all the earth, and every tree with seed in its fruit. You shall have them for food. And to every beast of the earth and to every bird of the heavens and to everything that creeps on the earth, everything that has the breath of life, I have given every green plant for food.' And it was so. And God saw everything that he had made, and behold, it was very good. And there was evening and there was morning, the sixth day.

On day six God made every other creature that lived on the earth. Things that ran and galloped, slithered and crawled, spun and weaved, jumped and burrowed. There were cows and beetles, cats and foxes, badgers and deer, elephants and zebras, every living creature imaginable were suddenly roaming the earth. And then of course ... God made a man and a woman. Adam and Eve.

You'll notice that the creation of the man and woman are a little different to the creation of the livestock or the sea creatures or the winged birds. We'll look at that a little more soon. But there's one more thing that we need to see. At the end of almost every day, God surveys His handiwork and sees that it is good!

But wait, there's more!

What other principles can we learn from Scripture?

We see that the creation of man and woman looked a little different to the creation of other living things. Look at the verses below and see where the difference starts.

> *Then God said, 'Let us make man in our image, after our likeness. And let them have dominion over the fish of the sea and over the birds of the heavens and over the livestock and over all the earth and over every creeping thing that creeps on the earth.'*
>
> *So God created man in his own image, in the image of God he created him; male and female he created them.*
>
> *And God blessed them. And God said to them, 'Be fruitful and multiply and fill the earth and subdue it, and have dominion over the fish of the sea and over the birds of the heavens and over every living thing that moves on the earth.'*
>
> —Genesis 1:26-27

The first difference that we can see is that God made man 'in his own image' and after His 'likeness'. That means that we are image bearers of God. We were made to reflect many of the same attributes that God has – although not fully, because we are not God, and not perfectly because sin has made us imperfect. We are relational (meaning that there is a connectedness about humans that draws us to each other to love, care for, serve, and dwell with each other).

▼ *more...*

When Adam was made, he was also like God in that initially he was sinless. Does it mean that we look like God? No, because God the Father is Spirit and cannot be seen. However, we know that Jesus took upon Himself a human body and so yes, perhaps we could say that there is a likeness there!

The second difference that we can see is that God gave man (meaning man and woman) dominion over all the other living things. 'Having dominion over' just means to have guardianship or stewardship over. It means that we are God's representative on earth to keep order and rule. But it does also mean something else which is perhaps not politically correct in our culture today. When God gave man dominion over all the living things, He created a hierarchy. Do you know what that means? It means that God made humans more important than other living creatures.

What did we learn about... Creation?

1. We've learnt that there is a battle for truth that began when Satan challenged God's Words to Adam and Eve by saying, 'Did God really say …' This challenge is now what we face too as Satan tries to cause people to deny God as the Creator of the world according to how the Bible states it.

2. We've learnt that God is truth and that His Word the Bible is spoken by Him exactly according to His will, so we can trust it, believe it and apply it to our lives.

3. We've learnt that God is eternal and the creation account is not a record of God's beginnings. God has no beginning. But the creation account is a record of our beginnings.

4. We've learnt that creation occurred over six literal twenty-four hour days.

5. We've learnt that God's creation of man and woman was special and different to His creation of other living things.

6. We've learnt that we are image bearers of God.

7. We've learnt that we are God's representatives on earth, having dominion over the earth and all things in and on and around it.

8. We've learnt that God created man and woman as more important than any other things He made.

Study Questions

1. What is the battle for truth? When did it begin and why does it still rage today?

2. We read in Genesis 1 that God the Father and the Holy Spirit were there at creation. Read the verse below.

   In the beginning was the Word, and the Word was with God, and the Word was God. He was in the beginning with God. All things were made through him, and without him was not anything made that was made.

   —John 1:1-3

   a. 'The Word' is one of Jesus names. What does this Scripture verse tell us?

   b. Is Jesus God? (How do you know from this verse above?)

   c. How were things made?

   d. Was there anything made without Jesus?

3. Read the following verses:

   For the wrath of God is revealed from heaven against all ungodliness and unrighteousness of men, who by their unrighteousness suppress the truth. For what can be known about God is plain to them, because God has shown it to them. For his invisible attributes, namely, his eternal power and divine nature, have been clearly perceived, ever since the

▼ *more...*

creation of the world, in the things that have been made. So they are without excuse.

—Romans 1:18-20

3a. These verses speak about God's judgement for those who have not repented of their sin before Him. What does their unrighteousness suppress?

3b. Man's unrighteousness suppresses the truth because that is Satan's evil scheme to have God dishonoured and man lost eternally. But man has responsibility in this too. Man suppresses God's truth because he does not wish to obey it, nor be held to account for what he knows and rebels against. But these verses from Romans 1 reveal something to us. Even though man tries to suppress the truth, God has in fact revealed truth clearly to them. How has he revealed it?

What do the things that have been made (God's creation) reveal about God to man?

These verses say that because God has revealed Himself in His creation to man, man is without excuse. What do you think that means?

Man is without excuse to agree that there is in fact a God who is worthy of all worship and honour. How about you? Have you agreed that God is worthy of your worship and honour?

▼ *more...*

> ## Let's Pray Together
>
> Dear God, how worthy you are of our worship. You are the God who spoke and this world and everything in it, around it, and on it, came into being. Thank you for the beauty that you have created. Thank you for the amazing animals and creatures, the stars and planets, the sun and the moon. Things that give light and things that dictate the seasons. All of these things were made by your great power and might. Your Word tells us that creation reveals you to us, your attributes and power and greatness. And yet, the battle for truth rages on in men and women who refuse to acknowledge your greatness. Open my eyes that I might behold wonderful things in your creation and indeed in your Bible. Draw me, draw men and women who are without excuse, to yourself so that you would be honoured. Amen.

IN THE BEGINNING, GOD CREATED THE HEAVENS AND THE EARTH. THE EARTH WAS WITHOUT FORM AND VOID, AND DARKNESS WAS OVER THE FACE OF THE DEEP. AND THE SPIRIT OF GOD WAS HOVERING OVER THE FACE OF THE WATERS.

AND GOD SAID, 'LET THERE BE LIGHT,' AND THERE WAS LIGHT. AND GOD SAW THAT THE LIGHT WAS GOOD. AND GOD SEPARATED THE LIGHT FROM THE DARKNESS. GOD CALLED THE LIGHT DAY, AND THE DARKNESS HE CALLED NIGHT. AND THERE WAS EVENING AND THERE WAS MORNING, THE FIRST DAY (GENESIS 1:1-3).

MY ACTION PLAN

1.

2.

3.

4.

5.

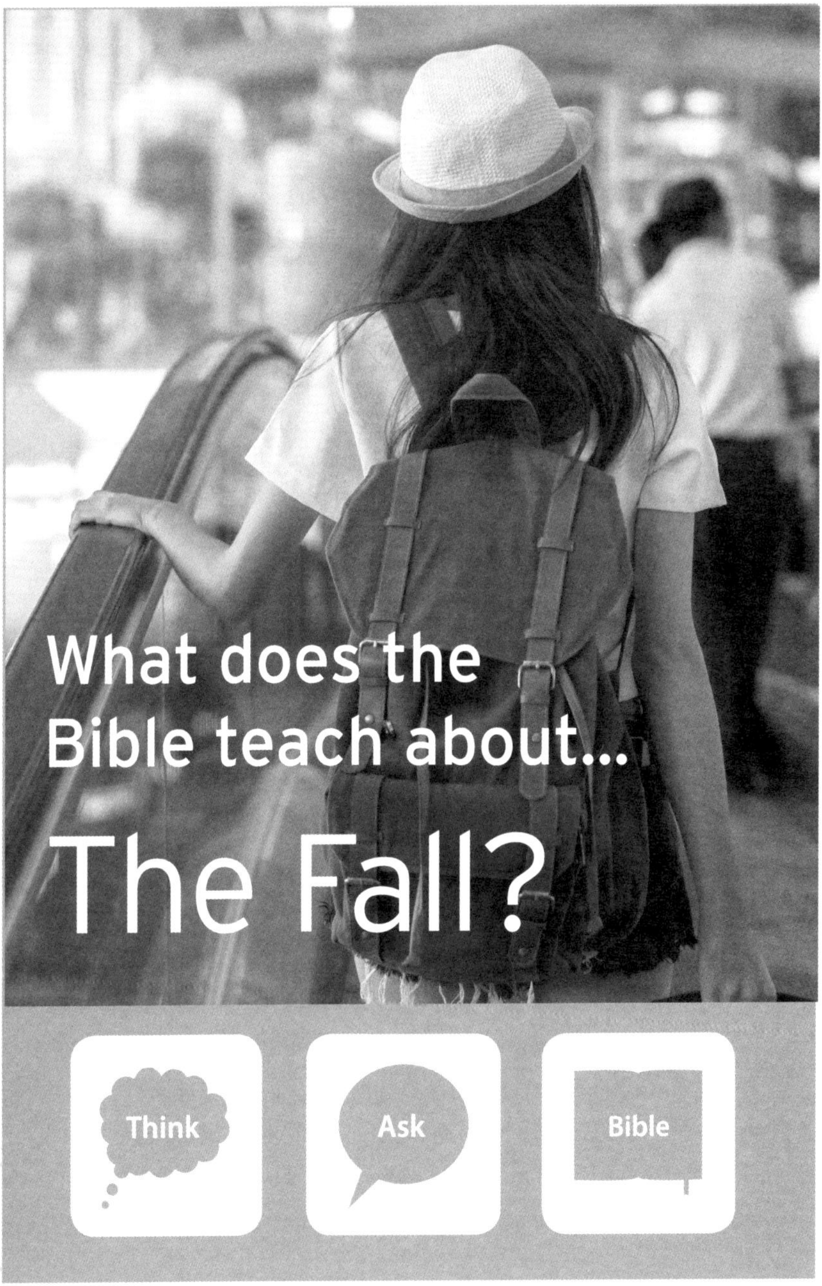

What does the Bible teach about...
The Fall?

Think

Ask

Bible

We have read the wonderful account of the creation of the world and everything in it. We see the special privilege that Adam and Eve had, as the first man and woman ever created, to have unique fellowship with God. Fellowship means close relationship, and in the Garden of Eden where Adam and Eve lived, they had the most beautiful relationship with God. In fact, God created Adam and Eve (and every person born since) to be 'image bearers' of Himself. This means that we bear the image of God in ways that animals and other created things don't. We have a soul which is eternal, we have intelligence beyond that of animals, we create and build and communicate and plan and love, we care for, serve and love one another. These things and more are a tiny reflection of the image of God. So, imagine, God the Creator of all things, and Adam and Eve, God's created children who bear His image, enjoying fellowship in the most beautiful place in the world. Could it get any better? No, it couldn't. It was perfect. But sadly it didn't stay perfect for long. Let's take a look at how the Bible records those beginning days of Adam's life.

The Creation of Man and Woman

These are the generations of the heavens and the earth when they were created, in the day that the Lord God made the earth and the heavens. When no bush of the field was yet in the land and no small plant of the field had yet sprung up—for the Lord God had not caused it to rain on the land, and there was no man to work the ground, and a mist was going up from the land and was watering the whole face of the ground—then the Lord God formed the man of dust from the ground and breathed into his nostrils the breath of life, and the man became a living creature. And the Lord God planted a garden in Eden, in the east, and there he put the man whom he had formed. And out of the ground the Lord God made to spring up every tree that is pleasant to the sight and good for food. The tree of life was in the midst of the garden, and the tree of the knowledge of good and evil. A river flowed out of Eden to water the garden, and there it divided and became four rivers. The name of the first is the Pishon. It is the one that flowed around the whole land of Havilah, where there is gold. And the gold of that land is good; bdellium and onyx stone are there. The name of the second river is the Gihon. It is the one that flowed around the whole land of Cush. And the name of the third river is the Tigris, which flows east of Assyria. And the fourth river is the Euphrates. The Lord God took the man and put him in the garden of Eden to work it and keep it. And the Lord God commanded the man, saying, 'You may surely eat of every tree of the garden, but of the tree of the knowledge of good and evil you shall not eat, for in the day that you eat of it you shall surely die.'

—Genesis 2:4-17

We read that God formed Adam out of the dust of the earth and breathed life into him. God is the 'life giver' and life is a gift from God to us. We also read that God put the man to work in the garden that He Himself had planted. God who created the magnificent trees also became the first supreme landscape artist. It must have been a wonderful sight to behold. I wonder what Adam's response was when he first walked into the garden and took a look around him? I expect he was overwhelmed. And then perhaps he knew how blessed he was to be a gardener in God's magnificent garden. This was no ordinary garden was it? For a start, there were no weeds or thorns or thistles, although they would come later. But there were magnificent trees perhaps filled with birds while the air was filled with their song. There were rivers which were teeming with fish! Animals of every kind were nibbling at the grass, lying in the sun, drinking from the rivers. But, there was still a very important addition to be made in the form of a wife for Adam. God's love for Adam is so clear isn't it? Not only does Adam get to be an image bearer of God, and to have the privilege of being superior to any other created thing, and to be the guardian over all creation, but God also wants to make sure that Adam is not alone. God sees that Adam needs a helper and He presents Adam with a beautiful woman designed just for that role. How amazing! Adam and Eve must have both laughed with delight when they saw each other! Adam knew that this woman was already his best friend, his companion, one whom he would laugh with, work with and be in the perfect partnership with. And it was like that for a while.

So, Adam and Eve get on with their new lives together, working in the garden side by side as God had intended. But there is more to be considered. At some point God also created beings that are His special servants. We call them 'angels'. We read numerous accounts in Scripture of God's angels as His messengers (remember the angel Gabriel who told Mary she was going to have a baby). We also read in our Bibles about someone called Satan. Satan is God's enemy and his desire is to rule over God and over the world. Satan used to be an angel. It is likely that he was important and very beautiful, but the Bible tells us that he became proud and wanted to take over from God. So, God threw Satan and all of his followers out of heaven. Satan desired even from his fallen position to rule, so he came up with a plan. He would tempt man and woman into sin which would separate them from God. It was a cunning plan as he entered into the form of a serpent and approached Eve as she worked alone in God's garden.

> *Now the serpent was more crafty than any other beast of the field that the Lord God had made.*

He said to the woman, 'Did God actually say, "You shall not eat of any tree in the garden"?' And the woman said to the serpent, 'We may eat of the fruit of the trees in the garden, but God said, "You shall not eat of the fruit of the tree that is in the midst of the garden, neither shall you touch it, lest you die."' But the serpent said to the woman, 'You will not surely die. For God knows that when you eat of it your eyes will be opened, and you will be like God, knowing good and evil.'

—Genesis 3:1-5

> ### Did You Know ...?
> Temptation comes to all of us, but the Bible tells us that we can submit ourselves to God and resist the devil – and he will flee from us! (James 4:7)

Satan deceived Eve. He caused her to doubt God. He said to her, 'Did God actually say ...?' What Eve said was sort of right. God had said that they were to eat from the fruit of any tree except the one in the middle of the garden, the Tree of the Knowledge of Good and Evil. But when she said that 'touching' it would cause them to die – she was wrong. I wonder why she did that? Was it that Adam had told her incorrectly what God had told him? Or did they add that rule as a way to protect themselves from the temptation of eating it? Either way, it wasn't right.

But what was Satan doing when he quizzed Eve about what God had actually said? Was he testing her ability to recall knowledge? No. He was actually planting a wrong thought in her mind. He made her think that God did not love her because He was denying her the thing that would be so good for her. 'Did God actually say ...?' We could paraphrase that to say it this way; 'Does God actually love you the way He says He does? Otherwise why would He deny you this special fruit which will change your life for the better?'

Satan is crafty, isn't he! He knows that appealing to the pride of a person will often bring a result. What result is Satan looking for? He wants to cause people to fall into sin, moving them away from God and towards him! So, did his plan with Eve work? Yes, it did!

> *So when the woman saw that the tree was good for food, and that it was a delight to the eyes, and that the tree was to be desired to make one wise she took of its fruit and ate, and she also gave some to her husband who was with her, and he ate.*
>
> —Genesis 3:6

Eve was convinced. She believed Satan. The fruit surely wouldn't cause her to die! It was beautiful, it must be good to eat, and not only that, it would make her wise like God! What more could she want? So, she reached up and she picked the fruit. She put it to her lips and took a bite. Then Eve gave the fruit to her husband and he ate it too.

Eve was sadly deceived. She had committed the first sin in all of mankind because of her willing rebellion against God's command. Then she committed another sin. She knowingly caused her husband to sin against God with her. At this point we don't hear again from Satan. He had done his work. He had placed temptation right before Eve and she had chosen to throw herself headlong into it. We don't even hear from Adam. He did not rebuke his wife for her rebellion, nor did he remind Eve of God's great love for them as their Father and Creator, pleading with her to seek out God and confess her sin against Him. Instead it appears that Adam was just as convinced as his wife. They both believed that the supposed benefit of the fruit was worth more than a relationship with God.

This, my friends is the account of the fall. It was the time when a man and woman who were in perfect relationship with God, allowed their desires and ambitions to become more important to them than honouring the God who created them. As a result they fell headlong into sin. Sin is the word used for anything that we participate in which is rebellious towards God. Because of Eve and Adam's sin, you and I were born with a sin nature and we struggle daily with the temptation to sin against God in order to pursue our own selfish desires. But is this the end of this sad tale? No, absolutely not. Regardless of what Satan was trying to deceive Eve into believing, God is a loving Father who desires life for His children. And He had a plan …

But wait, there's more!

What other principles can we learn from Scripture?

So, what happened next? Did Adam and Eve become all wise and knowing like God? Did eating the fruit fulfil all their dreams and desires? Not at all!

Then the eyes of both were opened, and they knew that they were naked. And they sewed fig leaves together and made themselves loincloths. And they heard the sound of the Lord God walking in the garden in the cool of the day, and the man and his wife hid themselves from the presence of the Lord God among the trees of the garden. But the Lord God called to the man and said to him, 'Where

▼ *more…*

> *are you?' And he said, 'I heard the sound of you in the garden, and I was afraid, because I was naked, and I hid myself.' He said, 'Who told you that you were naked? Have you eaten of the tree of which I commanded you not to eat?' The man said, 'The woman whom you gave to be with me, she gave me fruit of the tree, and I ate.' Then the Lord God said to the woman, 'What is this that you have done?' The woman said, 'The serpent deceived me, and I ate.'*
>
> —Genesis 3:7

We read that after they ate the fruit, their eyes were opened, not to all the wisdom that they thought they would receive, but to their nakedness and they felt ashamed. When we sin, we should feel ashamed because our hearts which are rebellious towards God are exposed. Adam and Eve made themselves makeshift clothing to try and cover their nakedness, in the same way that we are often tempted to try and cover our sin through lies, deceit and whatever else we can grab to cover it up. But here's the thing – God is all knowing (Omniscient). This means that nothing can ever happen or has happened that God doesn't know about. He knows everything that will happen before it happens. In fact, He knew Adam and Eve would sin against Him before He even created them. But He loved them. He not only created them, but He had already organised a plan to rescue them and to truly cover over their sin in a permanent way. But Adam and Eve don't know this. They thought they could hide from God – until God came walking in the garden to spend time with them. 'Where are you, Adam and Eve?' called God (although He knew they were hiding, He was giving them opportunity to confess their sin and repent.) God came, not in anger but in love. Adam responds

▼ *more...*

with an excuse. 'I was hiding because I was naked and afraid.' Why didn't Adam tell the truth? Why didn't he say, 'I was hiding because I've done what you told me not to. I've sinned against you and I didn't want you to know.' So God gives Adam another opportunity to tell the truth. 'Who told you that you were naked? Have you eaten of the tree of which I commanded you not to eat?' At this point does Adam come clean and confess? He has messed up big time! Does he feel terrible about it? No, what Adam actually does is blame God, and Eve. 'This woman YOU gave me, SHE gave me the fruit of the tree, and I ate.' (emphasis mine). Oh Adam – I want to groan every time I read this response. Except that I can recognise myself here. There are times when I sin that I actually try and make an excuse about it too – I try and blame others, or I even try and blame God for putting me in a situation where I have chosen sin! We all do it. The Bible tells us very clearly that there are consequences for sin.

> *For the wages of sin is death, but the free gift of God is eternal life in Christ Jesus our Lord.*
>
> —Romans 6:23

When we sin, it's not a matter of it being just a little blip on the radar that soon disappears. Sin brings death. That's what Adam and Eve were told in the Garden. If they ate the fruit, they would surely die. Yes, they would physically die, but it's not just talking of physical death. It's actually meaning spiritual death. A death which means we are separated from God for all eternity. Unless … there was a plan. And there was. God knew that the only covering for sin that could ever result in true life was for someone to die on behalf of the sinner. We read that the wages of sin is death – so something

▼ *more...*

or somebody had to die. But in order for this to pay the price for all who would sin, the one who was sacrificed would have to be perfect and without sin; otherwise, they would need a sacrifice on their behalf too. Throughout the Old Testament men and women would sacrifice an unblemished lamb or goat, and the death of that animal would make the payment for the sin. But this was only because it was a picture or sign of the ultimate sacrifice that was still to come. God had the ultimate sacrifice planned as a once for all sacrifice. He would send His only Son, Jesus – His Son who had been with Him for all eternity – to come to this earth in the form of a man and to live without sin in order to die on behalf of sinners. This is why John the Baptist, upon seeing Jesus said, 'Behold the lamb of God who takes away the sin of the world' (John 1:29).

But that was a long way into the future beyond Adam and Eve's time. Right now God needed to deal with Adam and Eve. He told Adam and Eve about the blood sacrifice that would be made on their behalf by His Son. And He gave them hope.

Then the Lord God said to the woman, 'What is this that you have done?' The woman said, 'The serpent deceived me, and I ate.' The Lord God said to the serpent, 'Because you have done this, cursed are you above all livestock and above all beasts of the field; on your belly you shall go, and dust you shall eat all the days of your life. I will put enmity between you and the woman, and between your offspring and her offspring; he shall bruise your head, and you shall bruise his heel.' To the woman he said, 'I will surely multiply your pain in childbearing; in pain you shall bring forth children. Your desire shall be contrary to your husband, but he shall rule over you.' And to

▼ *more...*

Think. Ask. Bible. | God's Word and Your World

Adam he said, 'Because you have listened to the voice of your wife and have eaten of the tree of which I commanded you, "You shall not eat of it," cursed is the ground because of you; in pain you shall eat of it all the days of your life; thorns and thistles it shall bring forth for you; and you shall eat the plants of the field. By the sweat of your face you shall eat bread, till you return to the ground, for out of it you were taken; for you are dust, and to dust you shall return.' The man called his wife's name Eve, because she was the mother of all living. And the Lord God made for Adam and for his wife garments of skins and clothed them. Then the Lord God said, 'Behold, the man has become like one of us in knowing good and evil. Now, lest he reach out his hand and take also of the tree of life and eat, and live forever—' therefore the Lord God sent him out from the garden of Eden to work the ground from which he was taken. He drove out the man, and at the east of the garden of Eden he placed the cherubim and a flaming sword that turned every way to guard the way to the tree of life.

—Genesis 3:13-24

We see in these verses above that there were immediate consequences for Adam and Eve's sin. Adam's toil to provide food for his family would be hard. Eve's labour to bring children into this world would be painful. And there would be the struggle between man and woman over the role of headship – the woman would desire it, but the man who has been given it would need to stand firm in it. God spoke to Satan and revealed that one day there would be One who would be ultimately victorious over him and would destroy him (Genesis 3:15).

▼ *more...*

Then we read Adam's words which are curious. He has just been told that his life will be hard. And that he will one day die and return to the ground he was made of! So, Adam responds by naming his wife. Ummmm … does that seem a bit random? Well, it's not. It's actually beautiful. You see, at some point in this conversation, Adam repents. He realises what he and his wife have done. He understands that sin will now separate them from the God who made them, and he is remorseful. God, as an act representing forgiveness and true covering over of sin, kills an animal and makes clothes to cover Adam and Eve's nakedness. But Adam knows this kind of sacrifice to cover sin is temporary, and that one day there will be One whose sacrificial death will cover sin eternally for those who repent. And he understands that this sacrifice will bring life, life eternal to those who receive it. God is the giver of life. Adam knew that from the very first moment he took his first breath. And Adam knew that God had provided the way to eternal life through His Son. And he knew that this life would be born through the descendant daughter of his own wife, Eve. So Adam named his wife. He called her Eve, because she was (and would be) the mother of all living. Eve means 'life'. God created man. Satan tried to destroy man's relationship with God. But God, He had a plan. A plan which true to His loving kindness, brings life.

What did we learn about... The Fall?

1. The Fall is the name given to the series of events in which man and woman fell prey to the deception of Satan, and chose to rebel (sin) against God. Their rebellion caused separation from God and bought with it the wages of death.

2. God knew even before creation that man and woman would rebel against Him. But He is loving and kind and had a plan ready to rescue sinners. This plan would involve the sacrifice of His One and Only Son, so that all who would believe in Him would receive eternal life instead of the punishment they deserve.

3. No one is immune to sin. Because of Adam and Eve's sin we, as their descendants, are born into sin.

Study Questions

1. What was the lie that Satan told Eve in order to persuade her to rebel against God?

2. What is sin?

3. Why are we all sinners?

4. Is there anything that we are able to do as sinners to cover up our own sin and remove the consequences of sin? How do you know this?

5. *And you were dead in the trespasses and sins in which you once walked, following the course of this world, following the prince of the power of the air, the spirit that is now at work in the sons of disobedience—among whom we all once lived in the passions of our flesh, carrying out the desires of the body and the mind, and were by nature children of wrath, like the rest of mankind. But God, being rich in mercy, because of the great love with which he loved us, even when we were dead in our trespasses, made us alive together with Christ—by grace you have been saved—and raised us up with him and seated us with him in the heavenly places in Christ Jesus, so that in the coming ages he might show the immeasurable riches of his grace in kindness toward us in Christ Jesus. For by grace you have been saved through faith. And this is not your own doing; it is the gift of God, not a result of works, so that no one may boast.*

—Ephesians 2:1-9

▼ *more...*

5. What does Ephesians 2 tell us about ourselves from verses 1-3?

6. What do verses 4-8 tell us about God?

7. What can we see as being differences in Satan's plan and God's plan for us from the verses above?

8. How is it (from the verses above) that we are saved?

9. What word is used to describe salvation? And why is this word used?

Let's Pray Together

Dear God, thank you that you are rich in mercy and grace towards us. Thank you that even though Adam and Eve rebelled against you, that you had a plan to rescue not only them, but all who would receive you as their God. Thank you for your patience with us. You know the sin in our hearts and the rebellion that we express towards you yet you love us. Please help us to walk in obedience, to honour you and to resist Satan and his evil schemes. Amen.

SO WHEN THE WOMAN SAW THAT THE TREE WAS GOOD FOR FOOD, AND THAT IT WAS A DELIGHT TO THE EYES, AND THAT THE TREE WAS TO BE DESIRED TO MAKE ONE WISE, SHE TOOK OF ITS FRUIT AND ATE, AND SHE ALSO GAVE SOME TO HER HUSBAND WHO WAS WITH HER, AND HE ATE (GENESIS 3:6).

MY ACTION PLAN

1.

2.

3.

4.

5.

What does the Bible teach about...

Languages?

- Think
- Ask
- Bible

Bonjour! Ciao! Hola! Guten tag! Gidday! Namaste! Konnichiwa! Merhaba! Jambo! Ni Hau! Kia ora! Hello!

Each of these words above represents a different cultural greeting. We see French, Italian, Spanish, German, Kiwi/Australian, Hindi, Japanese, Turkish, Swahili, Mandarin, Maori, and English. You might know some of these or even use some of these in your family or school. But we understand that these words are just more than a cultural greeting, don't we? They point to the fact that each of these cultures has a different language.

> ### Did You Know ...?
> There are over 2,700 languages in the world and over 7,000 including local dialects!

It's fun to hear different languages, isn't it? Before our children were born, my husband and I went to Paris. We were very excited about being tourists in France and so we did what many tourists do – we jumped on a City Bus Tour. It was the middle of winter and it was freezing! Even so, we climbed up the stairs of the open top double decker bus and, shivering, took our seats. We put the headphones on which were connected to a speaker system, and we scrolled through the available languages until we came to 'English'. So, there we were, sitting with other people from all over the world as we toured the beautiful city of Paris, each of us listening to facts about the city in our own languages. It was so fun, and every so often I would scroll down to another language just to see what it sounded like. I learnt very little about Paris, but it was hilarious hearing words very strange to my ears. When we were too cold to cope on that open top bus any more, we jumped off and headed to McDonalds. It was so crazy trying to order a Big Mac in our very poor French, however with much effort, pointing and waving our arms at the menu behind the counter, it wasn't long before we were happily munching on our French burgers.

But imagine if it wasn't fun. Imagine if we were desperate to communicate to those around us but we just couldn't. Imagine if those around us suddenly started speaking in different languages and none of us could understand each other. That might sound a bit far-fetched to you, but it actually did happen.

> *Now the whole earth had one language and the same words. And as people migrated from the east, they found a plain in the land of Shinar and settled there. And they said to one another, 'Come, let us make bricks, and burn them thoroughly.' And they had brick for stone, and bitumen for mortar. Then they said, 'Come, let us build ourselves a city and a tower with its top in the heavens, and let us make a name for ourselves, lest we be dispersed over the face of the whole earth.' And the Lord came down to see the city and the tower, which the children of man had built. And the Lord said, 'Behold, they are one people, and they have all one language, and this is only the beginning of what they will do. And nothing that they propose to do will now be impossible for them. Come, let us go down and there confuse their language, so that they may not understand one another's speech.' So the Lord dispersed them from there over the face of all the earth, and they left off building the city. Therefore its name was called Babel, because there the Lord confused the language of all the earth. And from there the Lord dispersed them over the face of all the earth.*
>
> —Genesis 11:1-9

So here we are, still in the book of Genesis. We've learnt about creation and the Fall. Now we are a little further along, in fact right after the flood. Do you remember what happened in the great flood (if not, go back and read Genesis 6-9)? The Bible tells us that as the population on earth increased through the descendants of Adam and Eve, wickedness also multiplied. God in judgement of the wicked hearts, decided He would destroy all the inhabitants of the earth. But 'Noah found favour in the eyes of the Lord' (Genesis 6:8), and He called Him to provide a way of rescue for all who would be saved from God's judgement. You perhaps know Noah as the man who built the Ark, and you would be correct. But what else would have happened while Noah was building the ark? People would have come and said, 'Noah, what are you doing?' He would have told them that he was obeying God. He would have said that he was building an ark, as God had commanded, because it would be the haven and place of rescue for his family during the flood which God would bring in order to wipe sin from the face of the earth. Noah would have been witnessing and testifying to others while he built the ark. He was telling them that God was bringing judgement on the wicked, and the only escape was to submit to God. Did anyone listen to Noah? Sadly, no. So, the day came, and God told Noah and his family to enter the ark. Then he brought to the ark the animals which would be needed to reproduce their kinds when the flood waters receded. And then He shut the door. When God offers rescue from sin, there is a point where the offer is removed and God's judgement occurs. This is what happened. The earth burst open and vast tsunamis of water roared over the lands killing everyone not on the ark. What a tragedy. The people were told, but their sinful hearts despised God.

Many days and nights later, the waters receded back into the depths of the earth. Noah, his family and the animals came out of the ark to begin their lives anew on the earth. God gave Noah and his family a command when they left the ark. He said that they were to, 'Be fruitful and multiply and fill the earth.' So that is what they did – kind of. Babies were born and the population grew in number. However, the people did not scatter over the earth as God had wanted. Instead they gathered as one group and stayed together. In their pride, they thought their way was better than God's way. And that is where we are at as we read Genesis 11. The people, as one large group, are moving from the East to a plain in the land of Shinar, and there they settled. Then they had another plan. They decided to make themselves a great city which would make them famous through the ages. It would draw glory to their own abilities and to their own great plans. But who should these people have been giving glory to? To God. They were arrogant. Their pride was becoming more and more of a problem. They did not worship the true God. They built a great city and then they made more plans for their own glory. They planned to build a great big tower that would be seen for miles around and again, that would point to their own great glory. Did it come about? No. God brought judgement on their sin. God saw the pride in their hearts and the determination of the people to have their own way. He knew the way to stop them was to scatter them and to cause them to be unable to communicate with each other. Suddenly the people found they were speaking different languages. They were confused! How were they to communicate? How were they to build their great tower? They couldn't. It was hopeless. So, the people scattered as God had initially intended them to. And as they scattered, the division between cultures was made according to the language the people spoke. If you've ever wondered how it came to be that different cultures spoke different languages, there it is. It came about because of the rebellion and pride of a group of people whose desire for their own honour and glory was the priority of their lives. Isn't that sad!

But wait, there's more.

What other principles can we learn from Scripture?

1. Language reveals our heart's condition

The good person out of the good treasure of his heart produces good, and the evil person out of his evil treasure produces evil, for out of the abundance of the heart his mouth speaks.

—Luke 6:45

When Jesus' disciple, Luke, wrote these words, he was comparing someone who is saved with someone who is not. The verses he writes before these refer to the fruit that a tree brings forth. He points to the reality that a good tree cannot bear bad fruit, and a bad tree cannot produce good fruit. It's a picture of the evidence of salvation. Those who are saved – you could also say, those who are in Christ – will produce spiritual fruit in their lives as proof of their salvation. Those who are not saved will produce fruit which points to their lack of submission to Christ in their lives.

Luke then goes on to make a similar comparison with how people speak and what it reveals about the condition of their hearts. Just like a good tree produces good fruit, a good (saved and transformed) person reveals the treasure of his heart by the words his mouth speaks. And similarly, a person who is not saved will reveal this by what comes out of his or her mouth. Do we mean that those who are saved will always talk about God and those who

▼ *more...*

aren't saved will be known for using foul language? No, although those things might be noticeable. The language of a believer will be consistently (although not perfectly) God honouring, preferring others, kind, submissive, gentle and life giving. Their conversation, regardless of whether it is about sports, school, or what to wear to your formal, reflects a desire that God would be honoured.

Luke also uses the word 'abundance' when he speaks of the heart. You could translate that word to 'overflow' – it describes how there is so much that some spills over. The way that this treasure spills over is through our words. Our language. The book of James in the Bible has much to say about the way in which we use language. It can be dangerous – he uses the metaphor of a fire which consumes. Words which are lies, gossip, slanderous, unkind, prideful, self-seeking are like the flames of the fire which cause great damage and pain to whom they are inflicted upon.

So, there are some questions which must then be asked. What does your use of language reveal about you? Does it reveal the treasure of the gospel in your heart, or does it reveal a heart which is without Christ? And what are the overflow of your words focused on?

2. Language is a vehicle for the gospel

For 'everyone who calls on the name of the Lord will be saved.' How then will they call on him in whom they have not believed? And how are they to believe in him of whom they have never heard? And how are they to hear without someone preaching? And how are they to preach unless they are sent? As it is written, 'How beautiful are the feet of those who preach the good news!'

—Romans 10:13-15

▼ *more...*

These verses above are referring to salvation. Just as we read in Romans 10:9, 'if you confess with your mouth that Jesus is Lord and believe in your heart that God raised him from the dead, you will be saved.'

Jesus is Lord and He came to this earth to die on the cross to pay for our sins. He was raised from the dead in three days. This is what you need to know in order to be saved. Someone needs to tell you this gospel; this good news. Right? And how is the gospel shared? By using language, either in the written or verbal form. What we also see in the above Scripture from Romans is that the one who goes out to others with the gospel is valued highly. Even their feet are considered beautiful. Do you consider the feet of your friends beautiful? No, I don't suppose you do. I don't think my friend's feet are beautiful either. But if I was unsaved and my friend came to tell me the gospel so that I might be forgiven and made alive in Christ, I would think her feet were beautiful for bringing her to me! See how the beauty is not actually in the feet – but in what the feet represent. The feet took the mouth to the person, and the mouth spoke the life-giving gospel. Language is the way in which the life-giving gospel is shared. Have you received the life-giving gospel for yourself? Are your feet performing that beautiful task of taking your mouth to others so that you can speak the language of the life-giving gospel?

3. Language used by a gifted preacher is a gift to all believers

I charge you in the presence of God and of Christ Jesus, who is to judge the living and the dead, and by his appearing and his kingdom: preach the word; be ready in season and out of season; reprove,

▼ more...

> *rebuke, and exhort, with complete patience and teaching. For the time is coming when people will not endure sound teaching, but having itching ears they will accumulate for themselves teachers to suit their own passions, and will turn away from listening to the truth and wander off into myths.*
>
> —2 Timothy 4:1-4

These words were written by the Apostle Paul to his young son in the faith, Timothy. Timothy was a pastor, and Paul was encouraging Timothy to stay true to his calling. You might think that in encouraging a young pastor, Paul might focus on things like: look after yourself, don't burnout, make sure you entertain the youth group, keep the people happy by choosing a mix of old songs and new in your congregational singing, keep people united in whatever way you need to. After all, those words of advice seem like that would be a sure way for Timothy to have an easy ride as a pastor. But that's not what Paul said. In fact, nothing could be further from the reality of Paul's words. The first thing he encouraged Timothy to make as a priority in his ministry was to preach the Word. That means, 'Teach the Bible.' Then he follows it up with specifics on how that was to be done. Preach the Bible … In season and out. That means when people are desiring to hear God's Word, preach it! And when they aren't desiring to hear God's Word, preach it! Then Paul told Timothy 'use the Word to reprove, rebuke, and exhort.' Perhaps you might not be familiar with those words, but they basically mean admonish, and encourage. What does Paul mean by this? He means that Timothy, as the one who was entrusted with the care of the souls in his flock, was to 'bring God's word to bear' on the people's lives. He was to use it to help them to see their sin; Use it to encourage and comfort

▼ *more...*

them in their trials and pain; Use it in order that they might grow in maturity and in Christ-likeness. You see, when God calls a man to be a pastor, he has a special and unique way in which he has wired them to communicate His precious Word to His children. We ought to be so thankful that God has created language to be used in this way for our benefit, and as always, for His glory.

4. Language is one of the ways in which believers can bless each other

Therefore encourage one another and build one another up.

—1 Thessalonians 5:11

We've already mentioned the dangerous ways in which words can hurt not only one another, but also a Christian's testimony for Christ before unbelievers. Gossip, slander, lies, deceit all describe evil ways in which words can be spoken. But this verse in Paul's letter to the church in Thessalonica commands believers to encourage one another. That command applies to you and me too. So, how then can we use our language and words to encourage one another? My nana always used to say, 'If you can't say anything nice, don't say anything at all!' I think that's a good place to start. If the temptation is there to speak unkindly of something or someone, deny yourself the opportunity to indulge in sin, and instead zip your lip! But there's more we ought to do. We need to be encouragers. Paul didn't leave the Thessalonians without some guidance on encouraging one another. If we were to read further through chapter 5, we would see commands like: rejoice always, pray continually, give thanks in all circumstances, greet one another with kindness. Do you see that when we use our words in

▼ *more...*

these ways with and for one another, what an encouragement that can be? God was so kind to give us a way to express ourselves both to Him and to others. I think the main point to take from this chapter is to make sure that your words are intended for the blessing and encouragement of those around you. Don't you?

5. Language is one of the ways in which we express worship

Let the words of my mouth and the meditation of my heart be acceptable in your sight, O Lord, my rock and my redeemer.

—Psalm 19:14

Because your steadfast love is better than life, my lips will praise you.

—Psalm 63:3

In Psalm 19, the Psalmist makes a connection between the words of his mouth and the things he thinks upon in his heart. This shows us that words of praise from lips, while there is unrepentant sin in the heart, are not acceptable worship to God.

Psalm 63 shows us just one reason to praise God with our mouths. Because His love is better than this life.

6. Language is necessary for prayer

Pray then like this:

> *'Our Father in heaven,*
> *hallowed be your name.*
> *Your kingdom come,*
> *your will be done,*

▼ *more...*

> *on earth as it is in heaven.*
> *Give us this day our daily bread*
> *and forgive us our debts,*
> *as we also have forgiven our debtors.*
> *And lead us not into temptation,*
> *but deliver us from evil.'*

—Matthew 6:9-13

These words from Matthew 6 are Jesus' words to us. It's a guide for how we are to pray. Obviously the first thing to note is that prayer is a spoken method of communication between us and our Father in Heaven. The other thing we perhaps notice before we read Jesus' prayer is verse 9. He says, 'Pray then like this'. This tells us that there is a reason for telling us what and how to pray. If we were to look back at Matthew 6:5-8 we would see what the reasons are. In these verses Jesus is telling us how not to pray, and this includes not praying out of pride, so that others will be impressed by our big words or dramatic emotions. Instead we should pray in private out of sight of others. The other thing Jesus said is not to pray a heap of 'empty phrases' thinking that God will be impressed and therefore hear our many words. Just be yourself. Be focused, keep it simple, be quiet of heart, be clear in what you are saying. So, as an example of how to pray, Jesus gives us what we now refer to as 'The Lord's Prayer'. We see that Jesus begins praying by acknowledging that God is holy. Then He asks for God's will to be done above our own desires. We are to be thankful for God's provision and repentant of sin, and dependant on God's help to overcome temptation. This is a guide for things to include in our own prayer.

▼ *more...*

Sometimes though, we must acknowledge that our hearts can be so burdened with trial that we don't even know how to express ourselves in prayer. In these times, we can be so thankful for the Holy Spirit who intercedes (goes to the Lord on our behalf) for us.

Likewise, the Spirit helps us in our weakness. For we do not know what to pray for as we ought, but the Spirit himself intercedes for us with groanings too deep for words.

—Romans 8:26

But most of the time, we will be able to pray knowing what we need to say. Do you make the most of your language skills in order to have regular times of prayer with the Lord?

What did we learn about... Languages?

Ask

1. In the beginning days, there was one language for all people.

2. Many languages came about because the people disobeyed God and instead united to glorify themselves instead of God. So, God changed the words on their tongues and they were forced to scatter and establish communities around the same languages.

3. Language reveals our heart's condition and shows fruit of salvation or unbelief.

4. Language is a vehicle for the gospel. If no one goes to tell the gospel to others, how will people be saved?

5. Language is one of the ways that believers can bless each other.

6. Language is one of the ways in which we express worship.

7. Language is necessary for prayer.

Study Questions

Think

1. Sometimes we can be like the people who we read about in Genesis 11.

   Now the whole earth had one language and the same words. And as people migrated from the east, they found a plain in the land of Shinar and settled there. And they said to one another, 'Come, let us make bricks, and burn them thoroughly.' And they had brick for stone, and bitumen for mortar. Then they said, 'Come, let us build ourselves a city and a tower with its top in the heavens, and let us make a name for ourselves, lest we be dispersed over the face of the whole earth.'

   —Genesis 11:1-4

   We can use our language to unite together for a cause that is not in accordance with God's Word to us. Can you think of a time when this has happened – either in your life or in a situation in the world? What were the circumstances? What happened? In hindsight, was there a way this could have been avoided? How, or why not?

2. One of the most beautiful things that we can do with our language is to take it and use it to share the gospel. Write down below what you would say in sharing the gospel with someone who didn't know Jesus as their Saviour.

▼ *more...*

My son, if sinners entice you, do not consent. If they say, 'Come with us, let us lie in wait for blood; let us ambush the innocent without reason; like Sheol let us swallow them alive, and whole, like those who go down to the pit; we shall find all precious goods, we shall fill our houses with plunder; throw in your lot among us; we will all have one purse'— my son, do not walk in the way with them; hold back your foot from their paths.

—Proverbs 1:10-15

7. These words from Proverbs 1 are written from a father to a son. We have spoken of a category of words like rebuke, admonition, exhortation, warning. What category do you think these words from this dad fall into?

8. This dad's words are thousands of years old. They are warning about something that today we would call 'peer pressure'. What do you think the pressure is that the peers (so-called friends) might put on the son?

9. How are these words similar to the words of the people in Genesis 11:1-4?

10. The word 'come' – is used in many ways, but in both of these instances it was used for evil. Think about your own use of persuasive language (like the words 'come' or 'let's). Write down some ways in which you could use those words to worship the Lord or encourage others.

▼ *more...*

Let's Pray Together

Dear Heavenly Father, thank you for the words which we are able to use to pray to you. Thank you for your Holy Word the Bible which reveals you to us, and which points us to Christ and your gospel. Please will you help me to use language and words in a way which honours you, blesses others and furthers your gospel work. Please forgive the times when my words have been dishonouring to you, and have sought after attention to myself. Amen.

THE GOOD PERSON OUT OF THE GOOD TREASURE OF HIS HEART PRODUCES GOOD, AND THE EVIL PERSON OUT OF HIS EVIL TREASURE PRODUCES EVIL, FOR OUT OF THE ABUNDANCE OF THE HEART HIS MOUTH SPEAKS (LUKE 6:45).

LET THE WORDS OF MY MOUTH AND THE MEDITATION OF MY HEART BE ACCEPTABLE IN YOUR SIGHT, O LORD, MY ROCK AND MY REDEEMER (PSALM 19:14).

MY ACTION PLAN

1.

2.

3.

4.

5.

What does the Bible teach about...
Missions?

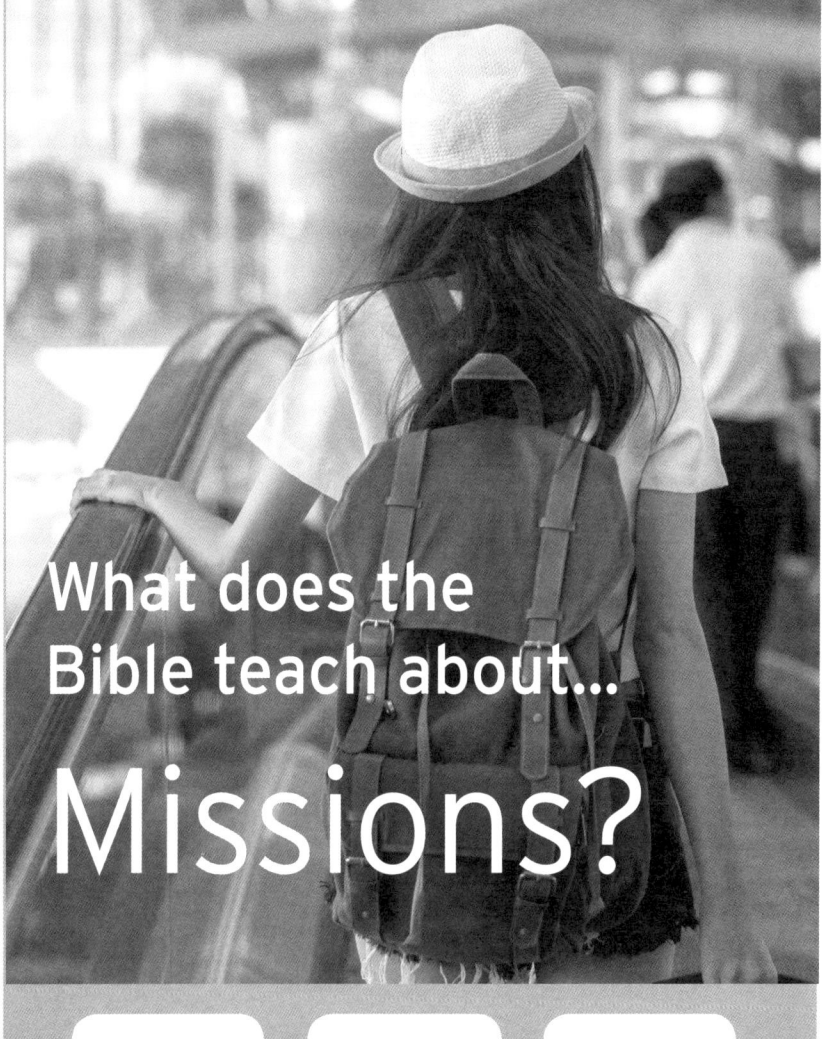

Think   Ask   Bible

Recently my husband finished reading a book about a man called William Carey. There are many, many books written about William Carey and soon I'll share why, but I thought you might be interested in a few facts about his life, so I had a quick look on Wikipedia to see what they said about him. William was born in a little village in England in 1761. He was from a reasonably poor family so his opportunities for education were limited and at age fourteen he began an apprenticeship in a trade. He worked with his hands and ended up as a cobbler (someone who repairs and makes shoes). But William was a very intelligent guy. He had a natural ability with languages and he also loved to read. He was inspired by the writings of American pastor and theologian Jonathan Edwards and the explorer James Cook. William married the daughter of his employer, Dorothy, and together they had seven children.

Now that sounds pretty unremarkable doesn't it, and in some ways the description of William Carey is similar to anyone born in a small village in England in those days. You can probably imagine the tiny cottages with only one or two rooms, jam packed with children and the poor exhausted mothers doing their best to put meals on the table and clothes on the children while the fathers were out from dawn till dusk working hard to provide for their families. But there is one way in which the Carey family was different. The Lord was doing a unique work in William's heart as he studied his Bible and other writings of pastors through the ages. William became known for his love of God's Word and very soon he was asked to preach in the local church on a regular basis. Then he was asked to become their pastor. And even during this time, William was writing his own articles and pamphlets concerning a sinner's need for the gospel of Jesus Christ. God was blowing into flame the embers in William's heart which would soon give him a concern for lost souls not only in his own village, but around the world. William became passionate about the need to somehow get the gospel to 'the heathen'. And that's what he ended up doing. In 1793, William and his little family boarded a ship and set sail to India where they stayed for the rest of their lives. This was not without many trials – sickness, poverty, the death of some of his children and eventually after a very long illness, the death of his own dear wife. And yet, through this time William continued to serve God in India. He learnt the local

> ### Did You Know ...?
> Adoniram Judson (1788-1850) served as a missionary in Myanmar. In the first twelve years there, only eighteen people were saved. But by his death he had established over 100 churches with over 8,000 members.

Indian languages so that he could translate the Bible into them. With a team of others, he assisted in the establishment of a college for local students, and even campaigned for the government to put a stop to some cultural traditions. Throughout his life in India, it would seem around 700 people were known to have been saved, but William's work in translation paved the way for many more. Because of his example, his desire to have the people of India hear the gospel and be saved, and his willingness to make any sacrifice in order for that to happen, William Carey became known as the 'Father of Modern Missions'. Many missionaries today have him as their example of one who took the gospel to the unsaved.

It might seem like an obvious question to ask, but let's ask it anyway. Why would a poor man in the 1700s care about the people of India? He had never been there, they spoke completely different languages, their culture and customs were totally different from what he was used to, and even the country was different. There were wild animals like tigers and dangerous snakes, and there were foreign diseases for which there was no treatment available. Even the food was completely different.

William Carey took his family to India because he loved Jesus and wanted to obey His commands. Look at the verses below.

> *And Jesus came and said to them, 'All authority in heaven and on earth has been given to me. Go therefore and make disciples of all nations, baptizing them in the name of the Father and of the Son and of the Holy Spirit, teaching them to observe all that I have commanded you. And behold, I am with you always, to the end of the age.'*
>
> —Matthew 28:18-20

These words are spoken by Jesus after his crucifixion and resurrection. He was with the disciples and he gave them this command, which we now call 'The Great Commission'. Notice that He first affirms His authority to the disciples. He reminds them that God has given Him all authority on heaven and earth. He was reminding them that in order to have this authority, He must in fact be the Son of God. He was affirming what we call His Deity (that He is God).

After affirming the authority that He has, He goes on to give this Great Commission. He had fulfilled God's mission for Him on earth and He was about to leave them and return to His Father. But now Jesus has a mission for all who are His disciples. This great commission is a call to evangelism. It's a call for Christian men and women to obey, wherever they are. It's the heartbeat of gospel mission. What do I mean by that? Well, let's look closer and see what this commission is all about. Let's look at some of the key words in this passage.

1. Therefore

My husband always says, 'Whenever you see a "therefore" you need to ask what is it there for?' And that's a great way to remember to look at what comes before, to find out why this command is being given. In this instance in the Great Commission, the 'therefore' is speaking of the authority that Jesus has been given in heaven and on earth. It tells us that we need to submit ourselves to Jesus' will for us. So here, Jesus reminds of His authority and then gives a command which must be obeyed.

2. Go

This word calls us to action, doesn't it? It's a verb or a 'doing word'. So already we know that this command involves some action on our part. Some people make the mistake of thinking that this word 'go' must mean that we need to leave where we are and go somewhere else, but in fact it actually just means 'as you are going about your regular daily lives'. The word GO isn't the key word in the Great Commission, but these next ones are.

3. Make Disciples

Ah huh! Here is the real command. If you are into grammar, you might like to know that this is the 'imperative command'. If you aren't into grammar, you just need to know that as you are going about your daily life, the Lord has called you to make disciples. What is a disciple? A disciple is a follower of Christ. Someone who has repented of their sin and believed in the Lord Jesus as their Saviour. In order to make disciples, there is one key element that we need. What is it? It's the gospel. The good news that tells us that we are all sinners, but God who is rich in mercy sent His beloved Son Jesus to die on the cross to pay for our sin so that we might come into a right relationship with Him.

To be able to share the gospel with others, there are a few things you need to know first.

- You need to know Jesus as your Saviour and Lord. Have you received the gospel for yourself?

- You need to know the gospel. Only when you know it can you share it. Very sadly there are those who share a 'watered-down' version of the gospel. Do you know what 'watered down' means? It means a weakened form. Let me give you an example. When my children were smaller, they used to love drinking orange juice. So, I would pour a half cup of juice for them and then fill the other half of the cup with water. It was a watered-down version of the real bottle of orange juice. Did it look the same? Mostly. Did it taste the same? No. Did they know about it? No! But now they are older, they can see me pour water into the juice and they ask me not to, because they know they love the taste of the juice without the water. They don't want the flavour of the juice weakened. Let me give you an example of how the gospel can be watered down.

When I was eleven years old, I went to a kid's summer camp. I had grown up in an unbelieving family, although I had the witness of my godly nana, so I knew about Jesus and my need for Him from a young age. Anyway, I was at this camp having a wonderful time. I loved the activities though the day – the swimming and the games and the meeting of new friends. And then I loved the Bible times in the evenings, where we would hear about Jesus. This one night, one of the speakers got my attention with a phrase that I hadn't heard before. He said that if we wanted to go to heaven when we died, we needed to ask Jesus into our hearts. This was a puzzle for me, but I went to my bunk bed that night and asked the Lord into my heart. And the next night I went to bed and I asked the Lord into my heart. And the next night … and the next night … and the next night … And on and on it went. I went home from camp tired out from all the activities, having had a great time with my friends, and … worried. What did this 'ask Jesus into your heart' mean? Did I literally just have to pray those words? Was there something I had to do to 'open my heart' for Him to come in? How did I know if He had heard me and was actually in my heart? Was I going to heaven when I died? You can see my dilemma, can't you? I had no one to talk to about this and so for months and months this was the thing that I prayed before I went to sleep every night. As I grew up, I heard this phrase used more and more at youth group and school (and I'm sad to say, I even used it myself because I was trying to talk the 'church language'). So, what was the big issue here? Firstly, I thought that asking Jesus into your heart was something I needed to do to become a Christian. Secondly, it didn't make sense to me on so many levels. Thirdly, no one checked in with me to see how I was going or to ask me if I had any questions. Fourth – and this is the most important thing – I was given a watered-down version of the gospel. Not at all in my memory do I have any recollection of being told about my sin and my need to repent and be saved – I'm not saying that the speaker didn't say it. But I am saying that even if he did, I was so distracted by the need to ask Jesus into my heart that I can't remember it. Since that time, verses such as Romans 10:9 have been a comfort to my heart.

If you confess with your mouth that Jesus is Lord and believe in your heart that God raised him from the dead, you will be saved (Romans 10:9).

Not only does it tell me what I need to do to be saved, it also gives me the reassurance that I need to know that I am saved!

Do you see that a phrase like 'asking Jesus into your heart' is a watered-down gospel? Here's the scary part – is that what the Bible tells us to do in order to be saved and know that we are going to heaven? No. It isn't. But what relief to know that the Bible does tell us clearly! We admit our sin before God, we ask His forgiveness and turn from the sin in our lives and we ask Him to help us to follow Him as our Lord for all of our days!

Be careful of adding in or leaving out parts of the gospel in order to make it easier or more attractive for people to hear. When you share the gospel to make disciples, give the whole gospel, the real gospel!

4. Baptise

Baptism symbolises dying with Christ to your old self and the raising up with Christ into the new life. It isn't a way of being saved, rather it is an outward act symbolising salvation. Various churches have different beliefs and practices concerning baptism. Speak with your parents or your pastor to find out what your church teaches.

Having been buried with him in baptism, in which you were also raised with him through faith in the powerful working of God, who raised him from the dead.

—Colossians 2:12

5. Teach

The role of a missionary or an evangelist does not end with someone being saved. The new believer needs to continue to learn and grow in their faith through regular teaching and studying of the Scriptures, and older believers need to come alongside them in this, to not only teach them but teach them to obey everything Jesus has commanded.

Earlier in our chapter I said that the Great Commission was the heartbeat of missions. Is missions work only for those who believe the Lord has a special calling on their lives to leave their home country and go into the world where they can take the gospel to unbelievers? No, missions work is for all of us. Wherever we look there are unbelievers who need to hear the good news of the gospel. The news that even though they are sinners and their sin has separated them from a Holy God, that God Himself sent His Son Jesus to rescue them from the penalty of their sin. Jesus died on the cross and paid for our sin so that we might receive Him as our Saviour. This is your mission. So … as you are going about your daily life, take this beautiful gospel with you, and share it.

But wait, there's more.

What other principles can we learn from Scripture?

I love reading biographies. The recorded true stories of real people, like you and I. There is always something to learn from someone else, either from what they did or didn't do, their attitudes, their character and personality, their dreams, goals, desires and priorities. I'm a pastor's wife so some of my favourite biographies are of pastor's wives and pastors and missionaries throughout the centuries. Reading about their families, their ministries and experiences, their friendships, trials and joys is not only an inspiration but a reminder of God's Sovereign and good hand in their lives. Biographies tell you about the person whom you are reading of, and they often reveal deeper things, like their love for their God, their sacrifices and willingness to obey without compromise. You perhaps even get a small glimpse behind the scenes into their private spiritual lives – their prayer lives, their time in the Word. And we can learn so much from this.

But does the Bible give us any of this? It certainly does. As we consider in this chapter the topic of missions, there is one person in the Bible who especially comes to my mind and that is the Apostle Paul.

Did you know that Paul was once consumed with hate for Christians? At this time in his life, his name was Saul. He was a Pharisee and you will read in the book of Acts that as a young man

▼ *more...*

Saul watched the stoning of Stephen (a follower of Christ). Saul was zealous in the wicked persecution of believers in Jerusalem, so zealous that he even travelled to Damascus with the goal of persecuting more believers. But something happened. On the road to Damascus Saul was confronted by Jesus. You can read in Acts 9 about Saul's dramatic conversion. He went from wanting to rid Israel of Christians, to becoming one himself! But even more than that – he became passionate that everyone might hear the gospel, repent of their sin and believe in the Lord Jesus as their Saviour. During his life Paul made many missionary journeys. Let's consider some of what Paul did as a missionary.

1. Paul prayed

And it is my prayer that your love may abound more and more, with knowledge and all discernment, so that you may approve what is excellent, and so be pure and blameless for the day of Christ, filled with the fruit of righteousness that comes through Jesus Christ, to the glory and praise of God.

—Philippians 1:9-11

In his letter to the church of Philippi, Paul expresses his love to them by telling them of his prayer for them. Paul prayed for the church that was growing and establishing. Notice that he didn't just pray for their physical needs, although I am sure he did that at times too, but he prayed for their spiritual needs. He wanted them to grow in spiritual maturity.

▼ *more...*

2. Paul preached God's Word

And on the Sabbath day they [Paul and his companions] went into the synagogue and sat down. After the reading from the Law and the Prophets, the rulers of the synagogue sent a message to them, saying, 'Brothers, if you have any word of encouragement for the people, say it.' So Paul stood up, and motioning with his hand said: 'Men of Israel and you who fear God, listen ...'

—Acts 13:14b-16

We see in these verses that Paul is being asked to bring some encouragement to the people. So, he stands and speaks. From Acts 13:16-41, Paul gives the people encouragement from the Word of God. He reminds them of God's faithfulness to His people. He tells them of Old Testament prophecies that were fulfilled and then brings them to the promised Saviour. Paul affirms to them that Jesus was truly God's Son and that He has provided salvation for sinners. He warned them of the peril of not listening and taking heed of these things. Paul uses God's Word to bring the encouragement people needed. Believers were encouraged to remind themselves of God's faithfulness to them. For those who didn't believe, Paul presented very clearly the gospel and their need of it. Paul's missionary heart was to share God's Word with unbelievers and believers at any and every opportunity.

What happened after this meeting that Paul spoke at? Verse 42 tells us that the people begged Paul to return the next week and tell them this message again. The next week, almost the whole city gathered to hear God's Word.

▼ *more...*

3. Paul stood firm in the face of opposition

The account continues ... When almost the whole city gathered to hear Paul again speak of God, the Jews became jealous and they tried to stir up opposition. What was Paul's response to this?

Acts 13:46 tells us, *And Paul and Barnabas spoke out boldly, saying, 'It was necessary that the word of God be spoken first to you. Since you thrust it aside and judge yourselves unworthy of eternal life, behold, we are turning to the Gentiles.'*

They didn't cower or run away or even decide to just move onto the next place. They spoke boldly, rebuking the jealous Jews. Further on in Acts 13 we see that many Gentiles were saved!

4. Paul trained men to be leaders within the church

Wherever Paul went, it seemed that he had someone with him. The opportunity these men had was incredible. They got to watch firsthand the pastor/missionary at work. They saw him love the people, they witnessed his love for God and God's Word, they were a part of his daily ministry as he travelled around churches, planted churches, preached the gospel, rebuked, taught, encouraged, comforted and equipped people. Read the following from a letter Paul wrote to his young pastor friend Timothy.

First of all, then, I urge that supplications, prayers, intercessions, and thanksgivings be made for all people, for kings and all who are in high positions, that we may lead a peaceful and quiet life, godly and dignified in every way. This is good, and it is pleasing in the sight of God our Savior, who desires all people to be saved and to come to the knowledge of the truth.

—1 Timothy 2:1-4

▼ *more...*

Paul was reminding Timothy to instruct the Ephesian church to pray that those in positions of authority over them might be saved. Remember these folks were Christians in an age of intense persecution, and Paul knew better than anyone that those rulers needed to be saved! These letters, which were full of pastoral instructions, were essential to the encouragement and support of young pastor Timothy. Paul was demonstrating not only a love for Timothy, but a love for the church in wanting them to continue to grow in their faith after they are saved.

5. Paul loved the people

I thank my God always when I remember you in my prayers, because I hear of your love and of the faith that you have toward the Lord Jesus and for all the saints, and I pray that the sharing of your faith may become effective for the full knowledge of every good thing that is in us for the sake of Christ. For I have derived much joy and comfort from your love, my brother, because the hearts of the saints have been refreshed through you.

—Philemon 4-7

Paul was writing to his friend Philemon and we can see from Paul's words that he loved Philemon very much. He prayed for Philemon and thanked God for him. Not only that but he was filled with joy because Philemon himself had been a blessing to other Christians, and that made Paul very happy. Dear friendships like this are a rare jewel. Be this kind of friend! Be this kind of encouragement to those around you, especially to your pastor!

▼ more...

There are many more examples from Paul's life that point to his missionary/pastor heart. However throughout the New Testament we see that it wasn't just Paul but Peter, James, John, and others who made mission their focus. This should be our starting point too. When we consider what God has for us in life, regardless of whether it be right where you are or the other side of the world, remember to: preach the gospel, teach the Word, disciple those around you, oppose those who reject Christ, and love the people.

What did we learn about... Missions?

Ask

1. Jesus commanded that we all obey the great commission.

2. The Great Commission is not just about going somewhere to serve God. It means that wherever you are in life, you are to take the gospel to those who need it, and make disciples by teaching them God's Word.

3. God uses ordinary people like you, me and William Carey to achieve His gospel purposes.

4. In order to take the gospel to others, we need to know it and we need to present it clearly without watering it down.

5. The Apostle Paul was an example to us in how he lived his life as a missionary. He prayed for the church, not only physical needs, but their deep spiritual needs too. He took the gospel to those who needed it. He encouraged believers with truths from God's Word. He discipled and trained others to be pastors of God's church, he opposed those who rejected Christ, and he loved the church.

Study Questions

Think

Brothers, my heart's desire and prayer to God for them is that they may be saved.

—Romans 10:1

For 'everyone who calls on the name of the Lord will be saved.'

How then will they call on him in whom they have not believed? And how are they to believe in him of whom they have never heard? And how are they to hear without someone preaching? And how are they to preach unless they are sent? As it is written, 'How beautiful are the feet of those who preach the good news!' But they have not all obeyed the gospel. For Isaiah says, 'Lord, who has believed what he has heard from us?' So faith comes from hearing, and hearing through the word of Christ.

—Romans 10:13-17

1. The above Scripture is written by the Apostle Paul in a letter to the Romans.

2. What does Romans 10:1 tell us about Paul?

3. Paul is speaking of the people of Israel in Romans 10:1. It is amazing to see that he has gone from persecuting Israel to loving Israel, and desiring and praying for their salvation. Is this your heart's desire for anyone? Is there someone that you

▼ more...

need to ask the Lord to help you to love and reach out to, just as Paul reaches out to the people?

4. What does it mean to 'be saved'?

5. After reading through these words of Paul's, is it enough for us just to pray that people will be saved? Why or why not?

6. In order for people to be saved they need to hear something. What is it that they need to hear?

7. Why does verse 15 describe someone's feet as beautiful?

8. Obviously, the Lord does not call all of us to the foreign mission field, as He did to William Carey. Regardless of where you are in the world, there is a mission field around you. It might be within your family. It might be outside your front door with your neighbours, your school friends, your supermarket checkout operator. Think of one or two people you can specifically pray for, for their salvation, and ask the Lord to give you opportunity to share the good news of the gospel with them. Pray for them now.

▼ *more...*

Let's Pray Together

Dear God, thank you for the example of William Carey and his family who followed your call to serve you in India. Thank you for the love that you gave them for the people there, and thank you that a number of people were saved through that time. Thank you for the ways in which you gifted William Carey to serve you, and that he was willing to use his gifts and talents for your glory. Father, may you continue to call men and women and boys and girls around the world to take the gospel to those who need to hear it. Help us to look around us in our own communities, so that we might fulfil your great commission, and that people might be saved. Thank you that Jesus came to pay for our sins so that we might believe in Him and be saved. Amen.

AND JESUS CAME AND SAID TO THEM, 'ALL AUTHORITY IN HEAVEN AND ON EARTH HAS BEEN GIVEN TO ME. GO THEREFORE AND MAKE DISCIPLES OF ALL NATIONS, BAPTIZING THEM IN THE NAME OF THE FATHER AND OF THE SON AND OF THE HOLY SPIRIT, TEACHING THEM TO OBSERVE ALL THAT I HAVE COMMANDED YOU. AND BEHOLD, I AM WITH YOU ALWAYS, TO THE END OF THE AGE' (MATTHEW 28:18-20).

MY ACTION PLAN

1.

2.

3.

4.

5.

What does the Bible teach about... Charity?

Think   Ask   Bible

Charity: the act of extending neighbourly love to those who are in need

Perhaps you know the story of a young woman called Ruth, in the Bible. We don't know a great deal about Ruth – who her parents were, or what her life looked like. But we do know that she married a foreigner. This man had moved to Moab, Ruth's hometown, with his parents to escape the famine of Israel. Sadly, Ruth's father-in-law died. Then her own husband and brother-in-law died, and she was left with her mother-in-law and sister-in-law. The mother-in-law's name was Naomi. Naomi had no one else in Moab, so she decided to return to her homeland, to her own people. Ruth made the decision to go with her, even against the advice of Naomi, because she loved Naomi deeply.

But what to do once they arrived? Naomi knew. She sent Ruth to glean. Do you know what gleaning is? In Naomi's culture and day, gleaning was made available by God's command to help those who were poor and needed food. At the time of harvest, those who were reaping the crop in the field would purposefully leave some behind. After the reapers were done, the 'gleaners' would follow behind to gather up what was left, and they would take it home to provide for their families. In some areas, once vineyard grapes had been sufficiently reaped or gathered, the poor townspeople were let into the vineyard to glean the leftovers. Gleaning was a way in which God used the landowners to provide for those who had no family to help them. It was an act of charity (voluntary kindness towards others). Let's look at this 'law of gleaning'.

When you reap the harvest of your land, you shall not reap your field right up to its edge, neither shall you gather the gleanings after your harvest. And you shall not strip your vineyard bare, neither shall you gather the fallen grapes of your vineyard.

You shall leave them for the poor and for the sojourner: I am the L<small>ORD</small> your God.

—Leviticus 19:9-10

The book of Leviticus was written by Moses. It records the law that God gave Moses for the people of Israel. At the time God gave His people these laws, they had made their Exodus from Egypt and had probably been in the desert for around a year. The Israelites had lived for generations in a culture very different to their own. The Egyptians worshipped many gods instead of the One True God so it was necessary for God to guide the Israelites on matters of worship, loving one another, and how to live a life of holiness. The law of gleaning that we read about in the book of Leviticus is just one of the laws that God gave in order to help with this. Interestingly, in my Bible this law comes under the heading of *'Love Your Neighbour as Yourself'*. While that heading isn't actually part of the Bible (it's a heading that was given when the Bible was translated to help us categorise this section of the laws), it's a good way to understand why God wanted a gleaning law to be obeyed. Who was the law given to benefit? Leviticus 19:10 tells us that the gleanings were for the needy and the stranger. God knows that our hearts are naturally sinful and selfish, so he made a law to help us to love others. But there is a place in the Bible where the idea of loving your neighbour is spoken of.

And one of the scribes came up and heard them disputing with one another, and seeing that he answered them well, asked him, 'Which commandment is the most important of all?' Jesus answered, 'The most important is, "Hear, O Israel: The Lord our God, the Lord is one. And you shall love the Lord your God with all your heart and with all your soul and with all your mind and with all your strength." The second is this: "You shall love your neighbour as yourself." There is no other commandment greater than these.'

—Mark 12:28-31

The above conversation happened between Jesus and a scribe, one of the religious leaders in Israel. Once again, they were trying to catch Jesus out by asking him a question about Scripture. They hoped that his answer would reveal that Jesus was in error. Instead He gave them an answer which they could not argue with. One thing that we need to notice is this: Jesus said that loving God should be our ultimate priority in life, but the next thing we are to do is to love those around us as much as we love ourselves. Neither one of these are optional commands. As Christians we must make our first commitment and priority to love God with our heart, soul, mind and strength. Basically, that means we must love God with everything that we are. Does that mean that we are to just

> ### Did You Know ...?
> Jonathan Edwards, a pastor in the 1700s, wrote seventy resolutions for his life. One of them was this: 'Resolved always to do that which I shall wish I had done when I see others do it.' August 11, 1723

have this constant gushy mushy lovey-dovey feeling about God all the time? No. Let's have a look at what love is.

Love is patient and kind; love does not envy or boast; it is not arrogant or rude. It does not insist on its own way; it is not irritable or resentful; it does not rejoice at wrongdoing, but rejoices with the truth. Love bears all things, believes all things, hopes all things, endures all things. Love never ends.

—1 Corinthians 13:4-8

These verses are a description of biblical love. Not love as the world or the culture around us would describe it, but biblical love. Is there a difference between the two? Have a read of these verses and see what differences you can think of.

Did you have a think? Here are some things that I think are different about the way the world loves and biblical love. Worldly love would say … Love is a feeling. Love is something that you can't control. How I behave towards you does not define if I love you or not. My behaviour is just a part of me, and if it hurts you then that's just too bad. Love is conditional – if you don't think or behave in a way that I want you to, then I don't love you anymore. Love is finite – it sometimes just ends, and I just somehow stop loving you.

Do you see the differences? Firstly, Scripture tells us that love isn't a feeling. It's an action. Not only is it an action, but it's not dependant on anyone else. It flows from an attitude of selflessness in a Christian's heart. Love means that you prefer others above yourself. This is the love that we are to demonstrate towards God, and towards others. God's Word is always relevant. When God gave His laws to the Israelites thousands of years ago, one of the laws was with regard to charity: The act of extending neighbourly love to others who are in need. We see from God's command that charity flows from true love for others, and being charitable is an act of obedience towards the Lord.

But wait, there's more.

What other principles can we learn from Scripture?

And you were dead in the trespasses and sins in which you once walked, following the course of this world, following the prince of the power of the air, the spirit that is now at work in the sons of disobedience—among whom we all once lived in the passions of our flesh, carrying out the desires of the body and the mind, and were by nature children of wrath, like the rest of mankind. But God, being rich in mercy, because of the great love with which he loved us, even when we were dead in our trespasses, made us alive together with Christ—by grace you have been saved—and raised us up with him and seated us with him in the heavenly places in Christ Jesus, so that in the coming ages he might show the immeasurable riches of his grace in kindness toward us in Christ Jesus. For by grace you have been saved through faith. And this is not your own doing; it is the gift of God, not a result of works, so that no one may boast. For we are his workmanship, created in Christ Jesus for good works, which God prepared beforehand, that we should walk in them.

—Ephesians 2:1-10

In these verses we see the greatest act of love that could be expressed to man. God made us alive in Christ! We didn't do it, we couldn't do it, but Jesus Christ did it for us. Because of His great love for us, we have been enabled to receive the gift of salvation. We who believe in Christ, have gone from being 'dead in our sin' to being

▼ *more...*

made 'alive in Christ'. That is an act of grace towards us. (Remember, 'grace' is God's unmerited or undeserved favour towards us.) Now look at verse 10. Scripture tells us that we are the workmanship of God, created to do the good works that God has prepared for us to do. It's good for us to remember that when God made us alive in Christ, there was something that happened to our spiritual heart. It is something that we call 'regeneration' – which means 'made new'. God took our old life of sin and gave us a new life in which the Holy Spirit causes us to despise sin and pursue holiness. We thus began the process of 'sanctification' – of becoming more like Christ. As people who are God's workmanship, these changes of being made new and being made like Christ, enable us to go on ready to do the good works that God has for us. The first work must surely be to love God with all our mind, soul, heart and strength and the second work must be to love our neighbour as we love ourselves. Every time we perform an act of neighbourly love, we are involved in an act of Christian charity. Are there different types of charity work? Yes. Let's take a look.

1. Acts of neighbourly love (charity) towards other believers

And let us not grow weary of doing good, for in due season we will reap, if we do not give up. So then, as we have opportunity, let us do good to everyone, and especially to those who are of the household of faith.

—Galatians 6:9-10

▼ *more...*

The Apostle Paul was reminding the people of the Galatian church to not become weary in their good works, and especially to do good to those who are in the household of faith. The household of faith means 'those who are Christians'. So, Scripture tells us that we must serve those within our church family (the local church family and even the international church family). What might that look like practically?

> *Honour widows who are truly widows. But if a widow has children or grandchildren, let them first learn to show godliness to their own household and to make some return to their parents, for this is pleasing in the sight of God.*
>
> —1 Timothy 5:3-4

We need to take care of our own families. In these verses, the church is instructed to let families take care of their widows and elderly parents. Obviously, some families don't live locally and aren't able to provide the care and help that is needed, and then the church is able to serve in whatever way is helpful. What can you do for these elderly folk? How about mowing lawns, making a meal or taking some baking to them? Or perhaps cutting wood or weeding the garden? All of these practical tasks, which are tricky for those who are physically weak, can become a burden. Your help can be a real encouragement. Or how about you offer to read Scripture aloud to them if their eyesight is failing? You can serve in very real and helpful ways.

▼ *more...*

> *Religion that is pure and undefiled before God the Father is this: to visit orphans and widows in their affliction, and to keep oneself unstained from the world.*
>
> —James 1:27

This verse from James is another way to care for those within the church. Visiting widows and orphans in their affliction (trial). The idea of visiting them isn't just to go and have a cup of tea and a scone, although that might be nice. It's the idea of going to them to serve them in their trial. This category of widows and orphans should also take into account solo mothers, children without fathers, folks whose spouses are unwell and need help to look after them, etc. The idea is that when there is a need within the church, we can and should offer to help in a practical way. Babysitting for the solo mother so she can have a time of refreshment, or sitting with a husband who has dementia or is bedridden so his wife can get a haircut or visit a friend, are acts of neighbourly love. And, remember, as our hearts have been made new in Christ, our natural selfishness can be put to one side as we imitate what Jesus would want us to do to show love.

2. Acts of neighbourly love (charity) towards those who are not believers

> *So then, as we have opportunity, let us do good to everyone, and especially to those who are of the household of faith.*
>
> —Galatians 6:10

▼ *more...*

We are to show neighbourly love (to show acts of charity) towards everyone. Why is that? Firstly, Jesus showed his love towards all people, didn't He? He healed people, He provided food, He showed compassion, He served them. And ultimately, He taught them the Way of Life. He gave them the gospel. He made a way for salvation for all who would believe. We are to follow Jesus' example in the way we love people, not only providing on a practical level, but also looking for ways to share the gospel and provide for their spiritual needs too. Does this mean that we should never just give money to an earthquake relief charity, or raise money for children in third world countries to receive an education? No, not at all. But that shouldn't be our only focus in loving our unbelieving neighbour. Pray for them too and ask the Lord for their salvation as your ultimate expression of love towards them.

What did we learn about Charity?

Ask

1. Christian charity is the act of extending neighbourly love to those who are in need.

2. Christian charity flows from a true biblical love.

3. Charity is the practical way of obeying God's command to love our neighbour as we love ourselves.

4. God has saved Christians from their sin and has created them to go and do the good works that He has prepared for them to do.

5. We are to show charitable acts to those who are Christians as an expression of love and care within God's family.

6. We are to show charitable acts towards those who are not saved as an expression of God's love for them and with the hope and prayer that they would be saved.

Study Questions

So, if there is any encouragement in Christ, any comfort from love, any participation in the Spirit, any affection and sympathy, complete my joy by being of the same mind, having the same love, being in full accord and of one mind. Do nothing from selfish ambition or conceit, but in humility count others more significant than yourselves. Let each of you look not only to his own interests, but also to the interests of others. Have this mind among yourselves, which is yours in Christ Jesus, who, though he was in the form of God, did not count equality with God a thing to be grasped but emptied himself, by taking the form of a servant, being born in the likeness of men.

—Philippians 2:1-7

In these verses, the Apostle Paul writes to the Philippian church to encourage them in their good works because of Jesus' example to them (and to us).

1. In these verses Paul contrasts two attitudes towards serving. What are the two attitudes?
2. We see Paul speaking here of Christ's humility. In what ways was Christ humble?
3. We see in verse 3 that Paul exhorts us to 'do nothing from selfish ambition or conceit, but in humility count others more significant than yourselves.' Selfish ambition means to do something in competition with others so that you come out

▼ *more...*

as superior. Conceit means thinking very highly of yourself compared to others.

– Why would people do things because of selfish ambition or conceit?

– What attitude does Paul encourage us to have as we serve others?

4. What commands should we apply to ourselves when we are serving others?

5. Servanthood is hard. It's humbling because often we are doing tasks that are menial or things that we really don't enjoy (and they don't tend to be tasks that make us look good to others either). Paul speaks of Jesus' humility in these verses. What can we learn from Jesus' example to us?

Let's Pray Together

Dear God, thank you for loving us so much that you sent your Son Jesus to die on the cross to pay for our sins, so that all who believe might be forgiven and saved. That is the most amazing act of love that could ever be shown to the world. Please help us to follow your example in loving others, and in doing acts of charity to serve them. Please enable us to have a humble heart, to think more highly of others than we think of ourselves and to serve willingly and joyfully. And when we serve people who don't know you as their God, please will you open their eyes to their need for you. May they see what we do as an expression of your love for them. Amen.

WHEN YOU REAP THE HARVEST OF YOUR LAND, YOU SHALL NOT REAP YOUR FIELD RIGHT UP TO ITS EDGE, NEITHER SHALL YOU GATHER THE GLEANINGS AFTER YOUR HARVEST. AND YOU SHALL NOT STRIP YOUR VINEYARD BARE, NEITHER SHALL YOU GATHER THE FALLEN GRAPES OF YOUR VINEYARD. YOU SHALL LEAVE THEM FOR THE POOR AND FOR THE SOJOURNER: I AM THE LORD YOUR GOD (LEVITICUS 19:9-10).

MY ACTION PLAN

1.

2.

3.

4.

5.

What does the Bible teach about... Society and Culture?

Think   Ask   Bible

Back in the book of Genesis, we read of a young man called Joseph who was a little unwise. He had these older brothers who he didn't really get on with. Partly the problem lay with Joseph's father Jacob. He loved Joseph more than his other sons because Joseph was the son born to him in his old age. Of course, the other brothers could see the favouritism and they were jealous. But Joseph didn't help things at all. You see, Joseph dreamed two dreams – the first was that he and his brothers were binding sheaves of corn in the field and his brother's sheaves came and bowed down to his. In the second dream, the sun and the moon and

> ### Did You Know ...?
> Society is a group of people who live together in the same geographical region. Culture means the things that define the society – like language, religion, foods etc.

eleven stars (which represented his family) came and bowed down to . Instead of keeping the dreams to himself, the Bible tells us that Joseph told his family about them. Not only did his father rebuke him for sharing this, but the brothers hated him even more for it. In fact, they thought enough was enough! The jealous brothers made a plan to get rid of him and eventually they sold Joseph to slave traders in Egypt.

Perhaps you are familiar with what happens to Joseph. He ends up working for someone pretty important in the Egyptian government and eventually makes such a great impression that he is promoted to a role which included planning for a famine which the Lord had warned him was coming. During the famine, Joseph's brothers come from Israel, needing food for their families. Joseph recognises them and eventually reveals himself to them. They ask forgiveness for their wicked act and

Joseph not only grants it to them, but has his brothers and their families move to Egypt where he is able to provide for them.

The Lord blesses Jacob's family after their move to Egypt. They multiply rapidly until soon they are looked upon not just as a family, but actually as a nation of people.

> *Now there arose a new king over Egypt, who did not know Joseph. And he said to his people, 'Behold, the people of Israel are too many and too mighty for us. Come, let us deal shrewdly with them, lest they multiply, and, if war breaks out, they join our enemies and fight against us and escape from the land.'*
>
> —Exodus 1:8-10

What was happening here? Obviously, the Israelites had increased in number so much that they were now a potential threat to the Egyptians. So we can assume that the Israelites were different to the Egyptians. Although they were a part of the Egyptian society in that they lived in the same place, they stood out as different because of their culture. Perhaps they wore different clothes, their hair cuts were different, they ate different food, but ultimately, they worshipped One God. The Egyptians worshipped many gods. Whatever the differences, this new king of Egypt obviously thought that there was a problem with having all these Israelites in his land. He was worried they might overthrow his rule and take over Egypt. But on the other hand, the Israelites seemed to bring blessing to Egypt. They were hard working people and built up wealth for themselves. The king certainly didn't want to lose the financial blessing that the Israelites were to his country, nor did he want to lose the hard-working ethic they had. So, he did a very wicked thing and he forced the Israelites into slavery. The next 400 or so years (Acts 7:6) were bitter for the Israelites and they cried out to the Lord for deliverance. You perhaps know how

God delivered His people, through the obedience of an Israelite named Moses. When the Israelites had crossed the Red Sea and were safe from the reach of the Egyptian army, something tells us that the Israelites had been influenced by the Egyptian society and culture. God gave Moses the ten commandments. Why? Because He wanted to remind and teach His people how they were to live, and of their need to pursue holiness. Sadly, while Moses was up on the mountain receiving the Ten Commandments from God, something was happening at the base of the mountain.

> *When the people saw that Moses delayed to come down from the mountain, the people gathered themselves together to Aaron and said to him, 'Up, make us gods who shall go before us. As for this Moses, the man who brought us up out of the land of Egypt, we do not know what has become of him.' So Aaron said to them, 'Take off the rings of gold that are in the ears of your wives, your sons, and your daughters, and bring them to me.' So all the people took off the rings of gold that were in their ears and brought them to Aaron. And he received the gold from their hand and fashioned it with a graving tool and made a golden calf. And they said, 'These are your gods, O Israel, who brought you up out of the land of Egypt!' When Aaron saw this, he built an altar before it. And Aaron made a proclamation and said, 'Tomorrow shall be a feast to the Lord.' And they rose up early the next day and offered burnt offerings and brought peace offerings. And the people sat down to eat and drink and rose up to play.*
>
> —Exodus 32:1-6

The people of Israel went to Moses' brother, Aaron, and revealed the state of their hearts. Firstly, they revealed that they had conformed to the Egyptian way of thinking about gods. The Egyptians worshipped many gods – and each god would represent different things – the god of the sun, the god of cats, the god of frogs, the god of creation, the god of fertility – it seems like there was a god for everything. The Israelites wanted gods to go before them as they made their way to their new home. The Israelites revealed that they believed it was the Egyptian gods who had delivered them out of Egypt (which doesn't really make sense does it?) So, Aaron then builds an altar and tries to mix the worship of the Egyptian gods with the worship of the true God – the God who had heard their cry and delivered them from the wicked oppression of the Egyptians. It is clear that hundreds of years of living in Egypt had conformed the Israelites to the Egyptian culture in ways they perhaps were not even aware of.

It's ironic that Moses was on his way down the mountain with the commandments, the first two which actually addressed this very sin.

I am the LORD your God, who brought you out of the land of Egypt, out of the house of slavery.

You shall have no other gods before me.

You shall not make for yourself a carved image, or any likeness of anything that is in heaven above, or that is in the earth beneath, or that is in the water under the earth. You shall not bow down to them or serve them, for I the LORD your God am a jealous God, visiting the iniquity of the fathers on the children to the third and the fourth generation of those who hate me, but showing steadfast love to thousands of those who love me and keep my commandments.

—Exodus 20:2-6

God already knew the state of the Israelites' hearts. He knew that they had been influenced by Egyptian society and culture. He knew they needed to know how to live for Him in matters of worship, relationships, and practical living.

The needs that the Israelites had are not something new to us. All of us live in societies where the dominant culture is to worship something or someone other than God. In the western world, it is most likely to be ourselves, money, possessions and glory, that have captured our hearts. Even Christians living in New Testament times needed to be reminded of their place within the societies and cultures they were living in. Read the following words that the Apostle Paul wrote to the Colossian church.

> *See to it that no one takes you captive by philosophy and empty deceit, according to human tradition, according to the elemental spirits of the world, and not according to Christ. For in him the whole fullness of deity dwells bodily, and you have been filled in him, who is the head of all rule and authority.*
>
> —Colossians 2:8-10

Philosophy is basically knowledge which guides our behaviour. The world's philosophies are driven by Satan who seeks to deceive people away from Jesus. When Paul describes what happens when we listen to the world's way of thinking he uses the word 'captive'. The idea is that you can become a slave to the world's empty knowledge. It will rob you of your joy and hope in Christ and it will not lead you to truth, but will keep you in error.

Jesus presents things a little differently. The following words are part of a prayer that Jesus prayed for believers.

> *I have given them your word, and the world has hated them because they are not of the world, just as I am not of the world. I do not ask that you take them out of the world, but that you keep them from the evil one. They are not of the world, just as I am not*

of the world. Sanctify them in the truth; your word is truth. As you sent me into the world, so I have sent them into the world.

—John 17:14-18

Do you see what Jesus is saying? He says that Christians are hated by the world because they are not of the world. Although Christians are born into the world just like everyone else, the fact that they are saved means that this world is only their temporary dwelling, but their home is in heaven with God. That means that the way we look at life is different from an unbeliever. We don't live for ourselves and for the 'here and now' – we live for the Lord and for eternity. Notice that Jesus doesn't ask for God to remove Christians out of the world, but instead he asks God to keep them from Satan. What does that mean? Jesus was asking for protection for Christians from Satan's deceitful ways. He wants them to be protected from falling prey to worldly ideas and ways of living. He asks God to allow Christians to remain in this world, being kept from Satan and his error, then Jesus prays for believers to be sanctified. That means, 'to be made more like Jesus'. Jesus knows that when Christians are in society and in cultures with different values, they will face temptations to conform. That's why Jesus prayed for believers. And that's why God gave the Israelites the Ten Commandments – so they would know the new ways that they were to live which would honour Him, instead of following the error that they had learned from the Egyptians.

But wait there's more!

What other principles can we learn from Scripture?

I appeal to you therefore, brothers, by the mercies of God, to present your bodies as a living sacrifice, holy and acceptable to God, which is your spiritual worship. Do not be conformed to this world, but be transformed by the renewal of your mind, that by testing you may discern what is the will of God, what is good and acceptable and perfect.

—Romans 12:1-2

The Apostle Paul had much to say to Christians about their place in their world, societies and cultures. This passage I think, sums up all his desires for Christians, wherever they are. 'Don't be conformed to this world.' It's pretty simple really, isn't it? But he doesn't stop at not being conformed to the world, Paul says that instead we are to present our bodies as a living sacrifice, holy and acceptable to God.

Sacrifice is a word that comes with all sorts of funny and perhaps weird ideas isn't it? Before Jesus came as the ultimate sacrifice to pay the price of sin, animals were sacrificed to make payment for people's sin. Is this what Paul is saying – that we sacrifice ourselves on an alter as payment for sin? No, obviously Jesus has paid the price for our sin, so it can't mean that. But it does mean that we are to dedicate ourselves to God, not just our soul but our bodies too, that we might live lives that are acceptable to God. Of course, we will still sin, and when we do we are to stop and confess, and enjoy his promise of forgiveness (1 John 1:9). The idea is that the general

▼ *more...*

pattern of our lives will be the pursuit of Christ and the denying of sin. Paul then goes on to tell us that this way of living is an act of worship. Isn't that neat!

But – well, how are we to actually live this way? Are there special things we should do which show our dedication to God? Yes, there are. Paul says that firstly we are not to conform to this world. That simply means, 'Don't become like the world'. How might we become like the world? Perhaps an example would be in the way we dress, dressing for attention, dressing immodestly, and seeking to make our identity in how we look. Or perhaps we conform to the world by choosing another priority on Sunday over being at Church. We can be conformed in the way that we think – perhaps in choosing to believe that the Bible is not God's authoritative Word for our lives, or in choosing to believe that the Bible has it wrong and man's wisdom has it right (think about things like euthanasia, abortion, creation science, gender identity). Whatever God says, this world will disagree with it, and we need to choose carefully who we will be like. And this is Paul's next point: Instead of being conformed to this world, we are to be transformed by the renewing of our minds which will enable us to discern God's perfect will. Do you understand what that means? It means that our minds are to be transformed, out of the world's thinking and into the thinking that enables us to understand God's will.

How do we have a transformed mind which enables us to know God's will? Only by spending time reading, studying and knowing God's Word. Here's an example.

A friend at school invites you to play volleyball over summer, every Sunday morning from 10:00 till 12:00. You realise there is no

▼ *more...*

way your parents will allow that, so you tell your friend. You friend is very quick to say, 'Wow, I would never let my parents tell me what to do on the weekend! And besides, you're so great at volleyball, you should totally sign up for this! You'll love it.'

Your response could go two ways:
You could say something like this… *'I know, it's such a drag my parents won't let me do stuff on Sundays! I must be the only kid in this school who doesn't get to play sport on Sunday! I'm going home right now to let my parents know that I make my own decisions!'*

Or you could respond like this...
'Actually, my parents have a responsibility before God for my good, and it's good and right for me to be at church with my church family on Sunday. Hebrews 10:25 tells us that "we should not neglect to meet together, as is the habit of some, but to encourage one another," and my family believe that going to church on Sunday is how we obey this. I really appreciate my parents wanting God's best for me, so as much as I would love to play volleyball, actually I would rather be at church on Sunday. Thanks for inviting me though!'

The first response would show that your thinking has been conformed to the way of this world. Western world culture is very much 'child led' in your generation, and many kids are in complete control of the family. But God's Word, the Bible, gives us a different way to think about this.

▼ *more...*

> *Children, obey your parents in the Lord, for this is right. 'Honour your father and mother' (this is the first commandment with a promise), 'that it may go well with you and that you may live long in the land.'*
>
> —Ephesians 6:1-2

Not only are children to obey their parents, but they are to honour them as well. To honour someone means to show them respect. The first response to the friend shows neither obedience or honour to parents. But the second one clearly does, and that is God's will for every child. The second response shows a life that isn't conformed to the world, and instead shows a mind that has been transformed by God's Word, which is a pleasing sacrifice to God.

Question: Is it easy to respond in a way that shows your thinking has been transformed by God's Word? Well, sometimes it's not. Sometimes it's hard and it will come with some difficult consequences. But remember what we read in Romans 12:2 – being transformed by the renewing of our minds is an act of worship.

> *I appeal to you therefore, brothers, by the mercies of God, to present your bodies as a living sacrifice, holy and acceptable to God, which is your spiritual worship. Do not be conformed to this world, but be transformed by the renewal of your mind, that by testing you may discern what is the will of God, what is good and acceptable and perfect.*
>
> —Romans 12:1-2

Your mission, whatever society and culture you live in, is not to be transformed by it, but rather to be transformed in your own life by

▼ *more...*

Christ, and so become an instrument of transformation within your culture.

> *And Jesus came and said to them, 'All authority in heaven and on earth has been given to me. Go therefore and make disciples of all nations, baptizing them in the name of the Father and of the Son and of the Holy Spirit, teaching them to observe all that I have commanded you. And behold, I am with you always, to the end of the age.'*
>
> —Matthew 28:18-20

What did we learn about... Society and Culture?

1. Society is a group of people living together in a community. Culture is the beliefs, customs and ways, of a people group within society.

2. We can live within society and be the same as the culture around us, or we can be different according to how God wants us to live.

3. Often, the dominant culture in society is not honouring to God

4. The Bible tells us that within the society in which we live, we are not to be conformed by it, rather that we are to be transformed by God's Word.

5. Our mission as Christians is not to be transformed by the culture, but rather to transform it for Christ.

Study Questions

1. Can you think of values that your society holds high which are contrary to (the opposite of) the Word of God? What does God's Word say about these things?

   Here's an example: The world promotes Euthanasia. The Bible however says, 'You shall not murder' (Exodus 20:13).

2. Are there cultural practices in your society/community/school which you are unable to be a part of because you or your family are Christian?

3. What does the Bible say to these things?

4. *Wives, submit to your husbands, as is fitting in the Lord. Husbands, love your wives, and do not be harsh with them. Children, obey your parents in everything, for this pleases the Lord. Fathers, do not provoke your children, lest they become discouraged. Bondservants, obey in everything those who are your earthly masters, not by way of eye-service, as people-pleasers, but with sincerity of heart, fearing the Lord. Whatever you do, work heartily, as for the Lord and not for men, knowing that from the Lord you will receive the inheritance as your reward. You are serving the Lord Christ.*

   —Colossians 3:18-24

▼ *more...*

- The Scriptures on the previous page, from Colossians 3, show us how God wants a Christian household to look like. What differences can you see between the way the world promotes how families should function and the way that God desires families to function?

- The word 'bondservant' we could translate to 'employee'. God is saying that employees (workers) should obey their bosses with sincerity of heart. Do you think that this is how most people would look at their boss? What do you think are the world's thoughts on bosses and workers?

- These verses tell us to work heartily (hard and well), as if we were doing the tasks for the Lord because our reward comes from Jesus. What do you think the world would say to that? Why do most people work hard? (What are they hoping to gain?)

- If we look around us, we can see that our society's idea of success is to make money, be famous, look good and have lots of stuff that others can't have (holidays, big homes, beach houses etc). None of those things are wrong, but the idea of these things making you successful is wrong. When you read the verses from Colossians 3, there is no mention of success. But there is a common theme. What is it? How is it so different from what society values?

▼ *more...*

Let's Pray Together

Dear God, thank you for where you have placed us to live. Thank you for the different things that we can enjoy about our societies, communities and cultures, for the things that are unique to different people groups which are fun, beautiful and different. Please will you give us wisdom to not be conformed to the world's ways, but instead to be transformed by the renewing of our minds according to your Word so that we might know and understand your will. Use us to be those who can bring transformation to those around us because of your gospel. Amen.

SEE TO IT THAT NO ONE TAKES YOU CAPTIVE BY PHILOSOPHY AND EMPTY DECEIT, ACCORDING TO HUMAN TRADITION, ACCORDING TO THE ELEMENTAL SPIRITS OF THE WORLD, AND NOT ACCORDING TO CHRIST. FOR IN HIM THE WHOLE FULLNESS OF DEITY DWELLS BODILY, AND YOU HAVE BEEN FILLED IN HIM, WHO IS THE HEAD OF ALL RULE AND AUTHORITY (COLOSSIANS 2:8-10).

MY ACTION PLAN

1.

2.

3.

4.

5.

What does the Bible teach about... The New Heaven and the New Earth?

Think   Ask   Bible

When I was a little girl of about five years old, my absolute favourite place to be was on the playground. I loved climbing and swinging and sliding and spinning – all the best things about the playground. And I remember very clearly one night crying in my bed and my Nana coming to me to ask what was wrong. I tearfully asked, 'Nan, will there be playgrounds in heaven?' You see, I knew I was a Christian, and I knew that when my earthly life was over, I would live in heaven. But I didn't know much about heaven. What would it be like? Would there be playgrounds there? (Obviously I didn't think about the fact that playgrounds might not always be so important to me, but at the time they mattered very much!) My dear Nan, who was perhaps more concerned about the fact that I should have been asleep, replied with a very vague, 'I don't know.' It didn't do much to satisfy my anxiety about how I was to have fun in heaven, but I knew not to ask anymore and instead imagined heaven to have the very best of playgrounds!

Let's have a look at what we can know from God's Word about heaven

When God created the heavens and the earth, He made the first man and woman, Adam and Eve, to live in the garden of Eden. However, sin entered this world through their rebellion against God. The Bible tells us that the wages of sin is death (Romans 6:23) and that part of the curse that came because of sin was that every person born would one day face death. Thankfully, God's rescue plan from these wages of death was to send His only Son that whoever would believe in Him might not perish but have eternal life (John 3:16). But eternal life where? We know that when Christians die, they go to heaven.

Let not your hearts be troubled. Believe in God; believe also in me. In my Father's house are many rooms. If it were not so, would I have told you that I go to prepare a place for you? And if I go and prepare a place for you, I will come again and will take you to myself, that where I am you may be also. And you know the way to where I am going.

—John 14:1-4

Jesus is speaking here to His disciples. They know Jesus is leaving them and they want to go to be with Him, but Jesus knows that the time isn't right. These men who He has trained, have a job to do – they need to take the gospel to the world. Instead, Jesus tells them not to be troubled about His departure. He tells them that He is going to heaven. It is where all believers who have passed from this life are. The Apostle Paul reminds us that for Christians, heaven is in fact our real home, and this life on earth is just temporary.

But our citizenship is in heaven, and from it we await a Saviour, the Lord Jesus Christ.

—Philippians 3:20

So, we understand that heaven is our home. But what is this concept, the New Heaven and the New Earth that we read about in the Bible?

Then I saw a new heaven and a new earth, for the first heaven and the first earth had passed away, and the sea was no more. And I saw the holy city, new Jerusalem, coming down out of heaven from God, prepared as a bride adorned for her husband. And I heard a loud voice from the throne saying, 'Behold, the dwelling place of God is with man. He will dwell with them, and they will be his people, and God himself will be with them as their God. He will wipe away every tear from their eyes, and death shall be no more, neither shall there be mourning, nor crying, nor pain anymore, for the former things have passed away.'

—Revelation 21:1-4

Jesus' disciple John wrote the book of Revelation. It's the record of a vision which God gave to John revealing how things will end. It tells us how Jesus defeats Satan and all his demons and how they are thrown into the Lake of Fire (Hell), and it tells us about the judgement of all who are not Christians. But it also tells us of the future for Christians. John gives us a glimpse of that in his vision. He speaks of a new heaven and a new earth because the first heaven and earth have passed away. John is speaking literally here. This earth and the heavens will be consumed by fire and God will make a new earth and a new heaven which is not tainted by sin. John also speaks of the new Jerusalem coming down to the new earth from heaven. It will be the place where all believers will dwell with God. What do we know about this place?

- **The Holy City of Jerusalem will be our home**

    This city will be beautiful (Revelation 21:18-21). The Bible tells us that the streets are made of gold and there will be jewels and precious stones inlaid which reflect the light and sparkle and shine. In fact, John describes the holy city as a bride adorned for her husband. Have you ever been to a wedding? If you have you will know that the bride puts a lot of effort into her appearance on that day. She usually will have a white dress which symbolises purity, and her husband-to-be doesn't generally see her that day until they are at the ceremony where they will make their commitment to one another. Sometimes when I go to a wedding I like to look at the bridegroom's face as his bride walks up the aisle. It's always wonderful to me because it's almost as if he is seeing her in a new light. She isn't unrecognisable as the woman he has grown to know and love, but she walks to him adorned with bridal beauty that he has never seen before, as she is now ready to become truly his. The eyes of the groom are usually filled with wonder and love and adoration as he awaits his bride. This is the picture that John gives us here. The Holy City of Jerusalem will be even more beautiful than that bride adorned in wedding clothes.

We also know from reading further on in Revelation 21 that the new Jerusalem will be very large, and in the shape of a cube – as high as it is wide. That's amazing to think about isn't it!

- **There will be no sea**
Perhaps this seems a strange statement to you about what heaven will be like. Some Bible commentators say that in this world now, the sea represents separation between the nations and that the lack of sea in heaven shows the unity of nations in the new heaven. I like this idea. We have many friends who are dear to us around the world and we cannot get to see them because the sea is in the way of being able to easily get to their homes – but it won't be like that in heaven. Precious ones will be there, and we will enjoy each other all the time! Not only that, but there will be no need to be separate countries and nations in heaven, because we will all be there united to bring our praise and worship to God for His Glory!

- **God will dwell with us**
We know that as Christians we have the Holy Spirit who dwells within us, and that in heaven, Jesus will live there in His glorified

resurrection body. But we mustn't forget that God the Father will be there. It's hard to imagine how this might be because no one has ever seen God and in fact God is spirit, so how will we see God? God told Moses that no man can see God and live (Exodus 33) but He did allow Moses to hide in the cleft of a rock as he passed by, and He allowed Moses to see His glory. What happened to Moses after this? His face shone, because God's glory is revealed in bright light. The people were too scared to come near Moses because his whole face shone so brightly. In heaven, there will be no sun or moon to give light because the whole of heaven will be lit with the light of God's glory. God is our light! We will have no need to hide from God or from the brightness of His glory, instead our new heavenly bodies will be designed to cope with what God reveals to us of Himself, and even to reflect that glory (Matthew 13:43).

These verses in Revelation 21 tell us that we will be God's people. All this life on earth, we pray to God as our Heavenly Father, just as Jesus also prayed to His Father. But in heaven, we get to dwell eternally with Him, to serve Him, worship Him and know Him in a way that we cannot know Him in this life. How wonderful to be living with God, to see Him and to worship Him and fellowship with Him!

- **There will be no sorrow, tears or sin in heaven**
We read in these verses in Revelation 21 that God will wipe away all tears from our eyes. Does this mean that we will cry in heaven? No, it means that there will be no reason for us to cry in heaven because God will have removed all things that hurt us. No more death, pain, sickness, sin, unkindness, sadness, grief, suffering – all these things are part of this life that we live now and come to us because of the curse. But these things will be gone from the new life.

Can we answer specific questions like, 'Will there be a playground in heaven?' No. God in His infinite wisdom has chosen not to reveal some things about heaven to us. But we know the important things don't we. We know heaven is a place where God will live forever with those who belong to Him. We know it is a place of perfect happiness, a happiness which cannot be marred or tainted by sin or sadness or death, or even the memories of these things. And we know how to get there – don't we? Do you? If not, why not pick up a Bible now and read John 14:1-6.

But wait, there's more!

What other principles can we learn from Scripture?

One day Jesus was sitting talking to a crowd gathered around Him. He spoke in parables, which you might have heard described as 'earthly stories with a heavenly meaning.' That means that Jesus uses things that we are familiar with in this life to describe things which are unfamiliar in heaven to us. Let's look at some of those parables and what we can learn about heaven.

- **The kingdom of heaven is a place for those who belong to Christ**

    Jesus tells a parable about a man who sowed good seed in his field (Matthew 13:30), but while the man was sleeping his enemy came and sowed weeds among the wheat that had been planted. Of course, what happened is that the wheat grew and produced grain, but alongside the wheat there were weeds which although they looked like the wheat plant, did not produce any grain for the farmer. The farmer instructs his workers to leave the wheat until harvest time when the wheat will be gathered and put into the barn and the weeds will be bundled and thrown into the fire.

    Let both grow together until the harvest, and at harvest time I will tell the reapers, 'Gather the weeds first and bind them in bundles to be burned, but gather the wheat into my barn.

    —Matthew 13:30

▼ *more...*

In this parable the enemy is Satan. The wheat that grows are Christians who have grown because of the gospel seeds that have been planted, while the weeds are those who belong to the kingdom of darkness, the unsaved. It's a warning to us all to be sure that we are saved, not just have the appearance of being saved.

Further on in Matthew 13, Jesus gives the parable of the net.

Again, the kingdom of heaven is like a net that was thrown into the sea and gathered fish of every kind. When it was full, men drew it ashore and sat down and sorted the good into containers but threw away the bad. So it will be at the end of the age. The angels will come out and separate the evil from the righteous and throw them into the fiery furnace. In that place there will be weeping and gnashing of teeth.

—Matthew 13:47-50

Again, we see the distinction between the saved and the unsaved. When the fishermen pull in the net, they bring in fish. But they know the difference between the fish that were good for food and the fish that were not good for food. The parable tells us that this is what will happen at the end of time. There will be a distinction and a separation between those who belong to Christ, and those who do not. The kingdom of heaven is for those who are saved.

- **The kingdom of heaven will be large!**
    In the parable of the mustard seed and the leaven (Matthew 13:31-33) Jesus speaks again of the seed of the gospel as being small, like that of the mustard seed or the leaven (yeast). But from its very small beginnings it grows large. The work of the

▼ *more...*

gospel might seem small and insignificant to us but the power of the gospel has enormous effect, and it will continue to grow and work its way through the world until God sees that it has done the transforming work that He desires.

- **The kingdom of heaven is to be treasured**
  The kingdom of heaven is like treasure hidden in a field, which a man found and covered up. Then in his joy he goes and sells all that he has and buys that field.

  —Matthew 13:44

  Again, the kingdom of heaven is like a merchant in search of fine pearls, who, on finding one pearl of great value, went and sold all that he had and bought it.

  —Matthew 13:45-46

This man knew the value of the treasure that he had found. In ancient times it was common for people to bury their treasures and wealth to prevent it from being stolen. Then they might perhaps have died without telling anyone about the treasure, and over time as people walk through fields, the treasure might become uncovered. Perhaps a man stubbed his toe on the box and when he opened it he knew that nothing that he owned even came close to the value of this treasure. So, he sells everything he owns to be able to buy the field and make the treasure his. Then we see the merchant in search of fine pearls, who found one pearl of such great value that he also sold everything he had to buy it. The kingdom of heaven is like that treasure these men discovered. Nothing else in our lives even comes close to being as valuable. This parable tells us that we must rightly value the worth of God's kingdom and so do whatever we need to in order to receive it.

What did we learn about... The New Heaven and the New Earth?

Ask

1. Heaven is the place where all Christians will live after they die.

2. All Christians belong in heaven, their citizenship is in heaven.

3. Jesus has done everything needed so that Christians can go to heaven.

4. After God has thrown Satan and his followers into the lake of fire, God will destroy the sin tainted earth and heavens and create a new heaven and earth for Christians where they will live eternally.

5. There will be a new holy city of Jerusalem on the new earth where all Christians will live and it will be beautiful.

6. God will dwell with man in the new heaven and earth.

7. There will be no sea, no separation of people.

8. There will be no sorrow, death, sin, tears or sadness.

9. The kingdom of heaven is a place for those who belong to Christ.

10. The kingdom of heaven will be large!

11. The kingdom of heaven is to be treasured.

Study Questions

And he opened his mouth and taught them, saying:
'Blessed are the poor in spirit, for theirs is the kingdom of heaven.
'Blessed are those who mourn, for they shall be comforted.
'Blessed are the meek, for they shall inherit the earth.
'Blessed are those who hunger and thirst for righteousness, for they shall be satisfied.
'Blessed are the merciful, for they shall receive mercy.
'Blessed are the pure in heart, for they shall see God.
'Blessed are the peacemakers, for they shall be called sons of God.
'Blessed are those who are persecuted for righteousness' sake, for theirs is the kingdom of heaven.
'Blessed are you when others revile you and persecute you and utter all kinds of evil against you falsely on my account. Rejoice and be glad, for your reward is great in heaven, for so they persecuted the prophets who were before you.'

—Matthew 5:2-12

These words are Jesus' words, as He taught a crowd of people who had gathered to hear Him. He speaks of a group of people who he calls those who are 'blessed'. He contrasts their life on earth with their eternal life.

▼ more...

12. Read verse 3. What do you think Jesus means by 'poor in spirit'? How can the kingdom of heaven be theirs? Think carefully about what you already know of those who belong to the kingdom of heaven to make sure your answer is consistent. What other scripture could you use to support your answer?

13. Verse 4 speaks of those who mourn over their sin. What is the comfort that they will receive that Jesus speaks of? What other scripture speaks to those of us who are mournful of our sin?

14. Verse 5 uses the word 'meek' which means humble. How would a humble person inherit the kingdom of God?

15. Verses 6-9 are also descriptions of those who are blessed. Reflect on these qualities in your own life? Are you among those who are called 'blessed' here? Why or why not?

16. Verses 10 and 11 speak of those who are treated badly because they are Christians. Can you think of any throughout history who these verses describe? What was their situation? How did they respond?

17. For those who suffer for Christ, they will be rewarded. Is their reward in this life?

18. These words spoken by Jesus, known as the Beatitudes, describe Christians. The only people who are truly blessed are those who know Christ. We've seen that heaven, and the new heaven and the new earth in time to come, is for those who are saved through faith in Jesus Christ as their Saviour. Does this describe you?

▼ *more...*

Let's Pray Together

Dear God, thank you for what your Word tells us about heaven, and in time to come, the new heaven and the new earth. Thank you that it will be a place no longer tainted by sin, and without the sorrow and burden of this life. Thank you that you will dwell there and that we will be your people there. Thank you for the clear warnings that only those who are yours will be there. May your Word sink deeply into the hearts of all who consider these things, that they might be certain to make sure of their place with you for all eternity. Amen.

MY ACTION PLAN

1.

2.

3.

4.

5.

CHRISTIAN FOCUS PUBLICATIONS

Christian Focus | Christian Heritage | CF4K | Mentor

Christian Focus Publications publishes books for adults and children under its four main imprints: Christian Focus, CF4K, Mentor and Christian Heritage. Our books reflect our conviction that God's Word is reliable and Jesus is the way to know him, and live for ever with him.

Our children's publication list includes a Sunday school curriculum that covers pre-school to early teens, and puzzle and activity books. We also publish personal and family devotional titles, biographies and inspirational stories that children will love.

If you are looking for quality Bible teaching for children then we have an excellent range of Bible stories and age-specific theological books.

From pre-school board books to teenage apologetics, we have it covered!

Find us at our web page:
www.christianfocus.com

CF4•K
Because you're never too young to know Jesus